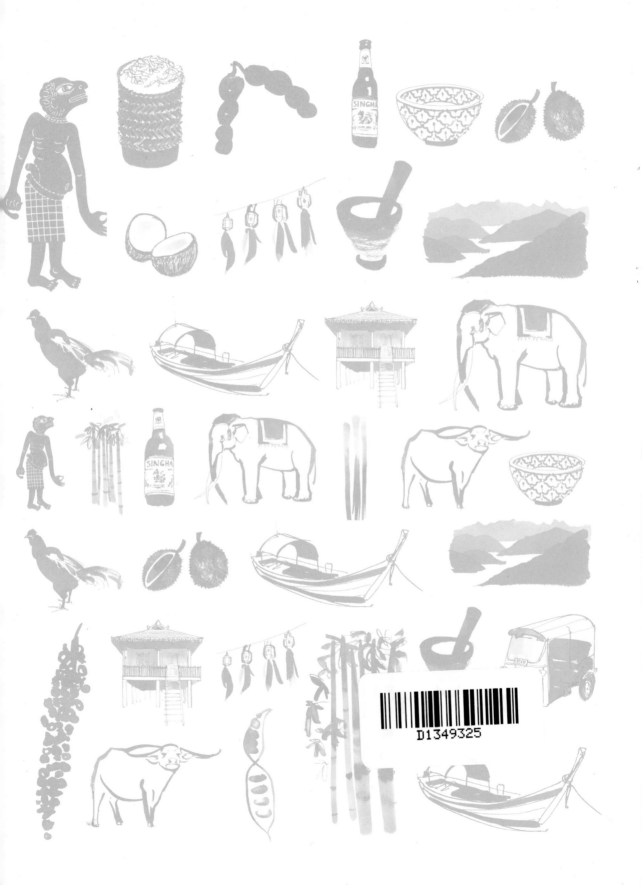

THAILAND
From the Source

*Authentic recipes from the
people that know them best*

Written and photographed by **Austin Bush** and **Mark Wiens**

CONTENTS

INTRODUCTION

The key to creating outstanding Thai food can be summed up in one word: balance.

Whether it's a creamy green curry, steaming *soup neua* or zingy *som tam*, all Thai dishes strive for that perfect balance of hot, sweet, sour and salty flavours, each one punchy without overpowering the others.

But while this delicate interplay runs through the expansive range of the nation's dishes, Thailand's culinary heritage is remarkably localised. Head north to the ancient cities of Lampang and Chiang Mai and the dishes you'll encounter bear witness to the region's relatively cool climate, with its mild seasonal food rich with bitter flavours. Further east, nearby Laos flaunts its culinary influence and, direct from the banks of the Mekong, freshwater fish dominates Isaan menus. Head for the beaches of the south and, unsurprisingly, seafood reigns supreme, while the chilli wields its might most heavily here too. And in Bangkok, the geography of the central plains, influences of the country's predominate minorities and the wealth of the royal palace have all served to shape the local cuisine.

But what doesn't vary, no matter which region you find yourself in, is the Thai people's emotional connection to food. Wherever they're found, these dishes signify history and heritage: a family recipe, created in the same way for generations, or a regional tradition, evolving with the twists and turns of geography and social history. The cult of food is an incredibly powerful theme to the Thai, for this is no fast-food cuisine: rich stocks bubble and simmer, patiently, for hours, while spices are pounded vigorously by hand, over and over, the better to draw out their complex flavours. And, come mealtimes, eating in Thailand is a communal affair, the food shared around the family table as the day's tales unfold.

Make no mistake: in Thailand, it's not just food: it's a labour of love.

COOK'S NOTES

This book aims to deliver Thailand's best local dishes – direct from the kitchens where they've been perfected and practised for decades or generations. Authenticity is at the heart of every dish we feature.

That means that some ingredients may be difficult to find in general stores. Most should be available in Asian supermarkets or online but, where possible, we have suggested possible substitutes too. The glosssary on pages 268–9 will help to identify unfamiliar ingredients.

It will come as no great surprise that authentic Thai food is incredibly spicy, especially to palates not accustomed to such fiery heat. Should you prefer a milder flavour, feel free to adjust the levels of chilli you find in the recipes. You may prefer, too, to deseed your chillies before cooking with them to remove a little of the kick from the chillies' heat.

In the spirit of authenticity, we have retained the chefs' original methods in these recipes. To make a paste, for example, you'll find instructions to pound the ingredients using a mortar and pestle, as the cooks themselves do. If you're short on time (or energy) though, you can use a food processor or stick blender instead.

The recipes in this book are designed to work in the context of a Thai meal, in which a number of dishes are served in the centre of the table for all to share. For a complete Thai meal with rice, four dishes – a relish with a few of its accompaniments, a soup, a curry (perhaps with a side dish) and a salad – will serve four hungry people. Some recipes are one-dish meals, such as minced pork and holy basil stir-fry (pages 67–9); the serving size on each page will reflect this.

For basic recipes for rices and other common dish additions, see page 264.

CENTRAL THAILAND & BANGKOK

Sophisticated, cosmopolitan food with royal, Chinese and Muslim influences

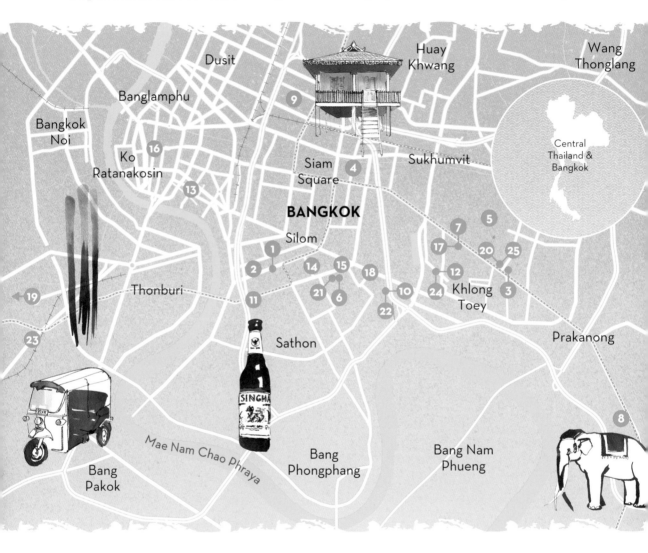

Dusit

Huay
Khwang

Wang
Thonglang

Banglamphu

Bangkok
Noi

Ko
Ratanakosin

9

Siam
Square

4

Sukhumvit

Central
Thailand &
Bangkok

16

13

BANGKOK

5

7

Silom

17

1

20

25

Thonburi

2

14

15

18

12

3

21

6

24

Khlong
Toey

19

11

10

22

Prakanong

23

Sathon

Mae Nam Chao Phraya

Bang
Phongphang

Bang Nam
Phueng

8

Bang
Pakok

1

THAI-MUSLIM
STYLE SALAD WITH
POTATO AND TOFU
Salat khaek

page 12

2

SATAY
CHICKEN
SKEWERS
Sate kai

page 17

3

GRILLED
AUBERGINE
SALAD
Yam makheua yao

page 21

4

GRILLED
BEEF
SALAD
Yam neua yaang

page 24

5

DEEP-FRIED
CATFISH & GREEN
MANGO SALAD
Yam plaa duk fuu

page 29

Source //
Khun Sanusi Mareh
Location //
Silom Thai
Cooking School

THAI-MUSLIM STYLE SALAD WITH POTATO AND TOFU

Salat khaek

Take the framework of a Western-style salad, add a dressing that blends chilli, curry powder and coconut milk, and you have this uniquely Thai-Muslim-style light meal.

Yam, or Thai-style salads, are an obligatory part of a balanced Thai meal. But eaten with rice, and typically revolving around meat or seafood rather than greens or vegetables, yam are consumed more like main dishes. More familiar to us in the West, both in terms of its ingredients and manner of serving, is *salat khaek*, 'Muslim salad', a staple of the Thai-Muslim repertoire in Bangkok and central Thailand.

Salat khaek (*khaek* literally translates as 'guest', a common yet somewhat derogatory word that's often used to refer to people of Muslim or South Asian descent) is a hearty, stand-alone salad that typically unites lettuce, hard-boiled egg, potato, tofu, onion and tomatoes, although these ingredients can vary. According to Sanusi Mareh, a Muslim and owner of Bangkok's Silom Thai Cooking School, 'Any ingredient can be used in *salat khaek* to make it more colourful, but it must include deep-fried potato chips.'

Another obligatory element of *salat khaek* is its unique dressing, which has elements of a Western-style salad dressing while also emphasising the sweet, rich flavours of Thai-Muslim cuisine. 'Unlike other Thai salads, the dressing here includes egg yolk and curry powder,' explains Sanusi, 'and it's also sweet, and creamy from coconut milk.' In terms of flavour, texture and appearance, the dressing served with *salat khaek* seems to occupy a place somewhere between an American-style salad dressing and the dipping sauce that accompanies satay, grilled skewers of meat, another Thai-Muslim standard.

And like Western-style salads, *salat khaek* can be eaten on its own, as a one-dish meal, but it's an excellent counterpoint as part of a larger Thai meal. If serving *salat khaek* as part of a meal, the salad's rich dressing means that stir-fried vegetables or a light soup might be a good accompaniment. *AB*

Serves 2 as a light meal

Preparation time: 45 mins
Cooking time: 15 mins

Ingredients
1 potato
400g block firm tofu, cut into thin slices
oil, for deep-frying
1 small head of lettuce, leaves separated
5 small cucumbers, sliced
1 onion, thinly sliced
10 cherry tomatoes
3 hard-boiled eggs, halved

For the dressing (makes more
than is needed for the recipe)
2 small dried chillies, deseeded and soaked
    in warm water
¼ tsp salt
60g shallots, finely sliced
1 tsp curry powder
2 hard-boiled eggs, yolks only
120g (4 oz) ground roasted peanuts
500ml (18 fl oz) coconut milk
3 tbsp fish sauce
80g palm sugar
4 tbsp tamarind sauce (see below)

1 First, prepare the dressing. In a mortar and pestle (or food processor), grind the chillies, salt, shallots and curry powder until you have a fine paste. Set aside.

2 In a medium-sized bowl, combine the chilli paste, egg yolks and ground peanuts. Set aside. Thinly slice the potato and soak the slices in a bowl of water and set aside.

3 In a medium-sized pan over medium heat, bring 250ml of the coconut milk to a simmer. Add the chilli-egg mixture, the remaining coconut milk, fish sauce, sugar and tamarind. Simmer, stirring to combine for about 5 minutes until the dressing thickens slightly. Taste and adjust the seasoning, if necessary. Remove from the heat and allow to cool.

4 Next, drain the potato slices. In a large pan, heat enough oil for deep-frying over a medium heat. Fry the potatoes and tofu until crispy and golden brown. Drain and set aside.

5 On a serving platter or four plates, arrange the lettuce, cucumbers, onion, tomatoes, boiled eggs, deep-fried tofu and potato. Spoon the dressing over the mixture, toss lightly and serve immediately.

Tamarind sauce

Tamarind is an essential ingredient, offering a sour component to dozens of Thai dishes, and it comes in a few confusing varieties with similar names. The difference between tamarind pulp, tamarind paste and tamarind sauce is a little in the eye of the beholder. Any variety used in cooking is simply the shelled fruit, with seeds and tough fibres removed, and some water added to loosen it up. You can buy it as a block of pure shelled tamarind (sometimes still with seeds and fibres, which need to be strained out eventually) or as a pre-made sauce or paste, often called tamarind pulp just to confuse things. If using the block – which is recommended – it needs to be hydrated, usually with a ratio of about one part tamarind pulp to three parts warm water. Put chunks of the block in a bowl, add the warm water, and work it with the back of a spoon until the pulp dissolves into the water, making tamarind sauce. Strain out the seeds and coarse fibres if present.

SATAY CHICKEN SKEWERS

Sate kai

Thai-Muslim cuisine's signature dish: grilled chicken skewers served with a rich, fragrant dip and a sweet/sour relish of cucumber and chilli.

S econd only to the Chinese, Muslims are the most significant cultural – and culinary – minority in Bangkok and central Thailand. Thought to have first visited the country as early as the 14th century, Muslims brought with them a cuisine based on meat and dried spices that eventually made its way to Bangkok and central Thailand.

'Thai-Muslim food has Indonesian influences, as well as Malaysian and Indian,' explains Sanusi Mareh, a Muslim and owner of Silom Thai Cooking School, in Bangkok. 'It's often sweet and it's not spicy, especially when compared to central Thai or north-eastern Thai food.'

These flavours and influences are apparent in what is probably the most lauded Thai-Muslim dish of all, *sate*, skewers of spiced, grilled meat. Available at just about every market in Bangkok and central Thailand, *sate* is as adaptable as it is beloved, functioning equally well as a snack or light meal, at just about any time of day or night.

Sate can be made from any protein, but Thai Muslims tend to use (halal) chicken, which is enhanced with a mildly spicy marinade. 'The chicken needs to be marinated in coconut cream and spices to make it tender and to give it a tropical flavour,' explains Sanusi. 'Turmeric is added to give it more colour.'

Yet *sate* is much more than just grilled meat. 'The most important part of *sate* is the dipping sauce,' explains Sanusi. 'It must taste nutty from peanuts, sweet wand creamy from the coconut milk. It's made from a curry paste adapted from red curry.'

Another important yet oft-neglected element of *sate* is *ajaat*, thinly sliced chillies, shallots and cucumbers in a sweet and sour dressing. '*Ajaat* should be sweet and sour, from sugar and vinegar,' explains Sanusi. 'The cucumber is a break from the greasy chicken and dipping sauce.' *AB*

Source //
Khun Sanusi Mareh
Location //
Silom Thai Cooking School

SATAY CHICKEN SKEWERS

Sate kai

Serves 4 as part of a
greater Thai meal

Preparation time: 1 hr
Cooking time: 30 mins

Ingredients

500g (1 lb 2 oz) boneless chicken, sliced
into 5cm (2 inch) long strips
1 tsp ground coriander
1 tbsp turmeric
½ tsp ground cumin
½ tbsp curry powder
1 tbsp light soy sauce
120ml (4 fl oz) coconut cream
¼ tsp salt

For the dipping sauce (makes more
than is needed for the recipe)
120g (4 oz) red curry paste
120g (4 oz) roasted peanuts
500ml (18 fl oz) coconut milk
1½ tsp salt
50g (2 oz) palm sugar or brown sugar
1 tbsp tamarind sauce

For the cucumber relish
120ml (4 fl oz) white vinegar
2 tbsp sugar
¼ tsp salt
60ml (2¼ fl oz) water
1 large fresh red Thai chilli, finely sliced
1 large fresh green Thai chilli, finely sliced
4 small cucumbers, finely sliced or grated
2 shallots, finely sliced

1 In a medium-sized bowl, combine the chicken, spices, soy sauce, coconut cream and salt. Cover and marinate for 30 minutes.

2 Make the dipping sauce. In a mortar and pestle (or a food processor) pound the curry paste and peanuts until combined. Set aside.

3 In a medium-sized pan over medium heat, add 250ml of the coconut milk and simmer until the oil rises to the surface, add the curry paste mixture, stirring well to combine. Bring back to a simmer and add the remaining coconut milk, salt, sugar and tamarind. Taste and adjust the seasoning, if necessary. Allow to reduce for 5 minutes, remove from the heat and allow to cool. Transfer the sauce to a serving bowl and set aside.

4 To make the relish, combine the vinegar, sugar, salt and water in a small saucepan over medium heat. Simmer for 5 minutes until the sugar has completely dissolved and the mixture is slightly syrupy. Remove from heat, set aside and allow to cool completely. Once cooled, add the chillies, cucumbers and shallots and stir to combine. Transfer to a serving bowl and set aside while you cook the chicken.

5 About 10 minutes before you want to grill the chicken, soak 10–12 bamboo skewers in water (this will stop them from burning on the grill). Preheat the grill to medium-high. Thread the chicken pieces onto the skewers and grill, turning occasionally, for 5–10 minutes or until fully cooked. Serve the chicken skewers on a large platter with the dipping sauce and cucumber relish alongside.

GRILLED AUBERGINE SALAD

Yam makhuea yao

Smoky, fragrant, tart, spicy, salty and meaty: this salad of grilled aubergine and smoky bacon unites just about every desirable flavour in Thai cookery.

Like many Thai dishes, *yam*, Thai-style salads, take numerous forms. Simple to make and based around almost any ingredient, *yam*, perhaps even more than any other Thai dish, are subject to the whims and interpretation of the cook who's making them. Such is the case with the *yam makhuea yao*, a salad revolving around grilled aubergine, as served at Bangkok restaurant, Soul Food Mahanakorn.

The typical grilled aubergine salad is served with a dressing that exemplifies the ingredients and flavours of central Thailand: rich coconut milk, the sweetness of sugar, and spicy *nam phrik phao* (a chilli-based condiment sometimes known in English as chilli jam). 'Our dressing is different from the standard,' explains Eakachai 'Eak' Matthakij, a chef at Soul Food Mahanakorn. 'Ours is tart and salty, only a bit sweet – we use palm sugar, while most places use white sugar. We also add coriander root to make it more fragrant.'

Also veering from the norm are the sides that accompany the salad. 'The usual version is served with hard-boiled eggs,' explains Eak, 'but we use soft-boiled eggs, in which the yolks are like lava. And usually chicken eggs are used, but we use duck eggs, because they're richer.' He adds proudly: 'The normal recipe includes prawns and ground pork, but we use bacon, which we make and smoke ourselves.'

One aspect of the dish that remains unchanged at Soul Food Mahanakorn is its central element: grilled aubergine. 'When aubergine is grilled, it becomes more fragrant, sweeter, smokier and less bitter,' explains Eak. Other constants are the dish's intense seasoning and its inherent adaptability. '*Yam* are strongly flavoured, especially tart,' says Eak. 'Thai people eat *yam* at lunch, at night, any time! You don't even need to eat *yam* with rice, they can be eaten on their own, or as an appetiser, with beer or alcohol. Our *yam* has enough flavour to be eaten this way, especially because of the bacon.' *AB*

Source //
Khun Eakachai
'Eak' Matthakij
Location //
Soul Food Mahanakorn
restaurant

GRILLED AUBERGINE SALAD
Yam makhuea yao

*Serves 4 as part of a
greater Thai meal*

Preparation time: 45 mins
Cooking time: 15 mins

Ingredients
4–6 long green aubergines, pierced with a fork
8–10 mint leaves
small handful coriander leaves, chopped
handful crispy-fried shallots (see page 264)
2 duck eggs

For the dressing
2 tbsp palm sugar
2 tbsp fish sauce
4 tbsp lime juice
3 shallots, finely sliced
2 cloves garlic, very finely chopped
1 small fresh red Thai chilli, sliced
1 coriander root, diced finely
*6 smoked bacon rashers, fried until crisp,
  then crumbled*

1 Grill the aubergines until the exterior is charred and the interior is soft, about 5–10 minutes. Place the aubergines into a bowl and cover with cling film and set aside for 10 minutes. Peel the burnt exterior from the aubergines and cut the flesh into 4cm sections. Set aside.

2 In a medium saucepan over a low heat, combine the sugar, fish sauce, lime juice, shallots, garlic, chilli, coriander root and crumbled bacon. Allow to simmer until combined and slightly reduced. Remove from the heat.

3 In a small saucepan, bring the water to the boil and add the eggs. Simmer for 6 minutes and drain. Plunge the eggs into a bowl of cold water and peel when cool enough to handle.

4 Arrange the aubergine on a serving plate. Pour over the dressing and garnish with mint, coriander and the crispy-fried shallots, then serve with a side of duck eggs if desired.

*When aubergine is grilled,
it becomes more fragrant,
sweeter, smokier and less bitter.'*

'Eak' Matthakij

Source //
Khun Yupin MacLeod,
home cook
Location //
Bangkok

GRILLED BEEF SALAD

Yam neua yaang

Slices of smoky grilled beef and a vibrant dressing come together in this old central Thai recipe, which Bangkokian Yupin MacLeod says is becoming harder to find.

These days, Thai food is synonymous with spicy heat, but this wasn't always the case. 'Thai people nowadays like their dishes very spicy,' explains Bangkok-born home cook and caterer, Yupin MacLeod. 'But the seasoning of the dish shouldn't be too strong. In the past, Thais said that the upper class preferred lightly seasoned food, while the lower classes preferred stronger food!'

Social hierarchy aside, according to Yupin a balance of flavour should be everybody's goal when making *yam neua yaang*, a salad of grilled beef and cucumbers in a dressing that blends fresh chillies, garlic, sugar, fish sauce and lime juice. 'It's an old central Thai recipe, from the Bangkok era,' explains Yupin, of the dish. 'My grandmother made this exact recipe when I was growing up. People still eat the dish today, but the cucumbers are served on the side and the chillies are chopped, not made into a paste.'

Yet according to Yupin, the dish's central element, beef, has caused it to fall by the wayside: 'Nowadays, *yam neua yaang* is harder to find. Before, Thai people ate beef, but today few do.' Of the dish's main component, she adds: 'I use beef fillet. You could also used tenderloin, but other cuts are going to be too tough. Grill the beef as long as you like, rare or well-done. You can even boil the beef if you don't have a grill. If you don't have beef, you could use chicken or pork instead.'

Although, according to Yupin, achieving a balance of flavours in the dressing is the ideal, she admits that there are exceptions: 'If eating the salad on its own, such as a snack with beer, it should be spicier.' She adds, 'As part of a meal, I'd couple *yam neua yaang* with something spicy, such as a curry or a stir-fry.' *AB*

Serves 2 as a light meal

Preparation time: 20 mins
Cooking time: 20 mins

Ingredients

1 × 300g (11 oz) beef fillet or tenderloin
¼ cucumber, peeled, deseeded, and
*   sliced lengthways*
¼ onion, finely sliced

For the dressing

1 large fresh green Thai chilli, deseeded
2–4 small fresh red Thai chillies
3 cloves garlic, peeled
3 tbsp fish sauce
4 tbsp lime juice
2 tsp sugar

Optional garnishes

few lettuce leaves
1–2 tomatoes, sliced
sprig of mint
salt and pepper, to taste

1 Make the dressing. In a mortar and pestle, pound the chillies and garlic until you have a fine paste, or use a food processor. In a small mixing bowl, combine the paste with the fish sauce, lime juice and the sugar. Taste and adjust the seasoning if necessary. Set aside.

2 Heat the grill to its highest setting. Season the beef with salt and pepper. Grill until you have your desired doneness. Allow to cool briefly, then slice thinly and set aside in a large bowl.

3 Add the dressing, cucumber and onion, stirring to combine. Remove to a serving dish and top with the garnishes (if using).

'It's an old central Thai recipe, from the Bangkok era. My grandmother made this exact recipe when I was growing up.'

Yupin MacLeod

DEEP-FRIED CATFISH & GREEN MANGO SALAD

Yam plaa duk fuu

This beloved central Thai salad revolves around a pillow of light, crispy deep-fried catfish, the freshwater fish they love to feed at the riverside, feeding them in return.

Thai food is largely about balance; balance in terms of the meticulous seasoning of its dishes, as well as the way those dishes are served. 'A complete Thai meal should have a soup, a stir-fry and a salad,' explains Porntippa Rayanonda, owner of Bangkok's Klang Soi restaurant. And one Thai-style salad, or *yam*, that has balanced many a meal in Bangkok and central Thailand is *yam plaa duk fuu*, deep-fried catfish and shredded green mango in a vibrant dressing.

'It's a family recipe, from my mother, who was from Bangkok,' explains Porntippa, of the recipe featured here. 'It's a central Thai dish, but nowadays people across Thailand make it.'

As is the case with most *yam*, the seasoning of the dressing, in this case a blend of garlic, chilli, fish sauce, lime juice and sugar, is crucial. 'It should be tart, slightly sweet, salty and spicy – all four flavours,' explains Porntippa, before adding that, 'spicy makes it taste better.'

Yet perhaps the most important element of *yam plaa duk fuu* is the catfish, an ingredient common in the river cities of Bangkok and Ayutthaya and the lakes and ponds of central Thailand. It's prepared via a unique process of grilling, mincing then deep-frying. 'Catfish gets really crispy when fried,' explains Porntippa, 'it's perfect for this salad.'

In fact, when dried sufficiently and deep-fried properly, not only does the catfish get crispy, but its abundant collagen causes the flakes of fish, along with a bit of help from the cook, to come together as one when deep-fried, resulting in a light, crispy layer that's perfect for absorbing the flavours of the dressing while still remaining crisp.

'*Yam plaa duk fuu* is eaten as part of a Thai meal, but some people eat it as an appetiser,' explains Porntippa. 'In a meal it would be good with a stir-fry, such as chicken fried with cashew nuts, or a soup. It's already a bit spicy, so you don't want to couple it with anything that's too hot.' *AB*

Source //
Khun Porntippa Rayanonda
Location //
Klang Soi restaurant

DEEP-FRIED CATFISH & GREEN MANGO SALAD

Yam plaa duk fuu

Serves 4 as part of a greater Thai meal

Preparation time: 1 hr
Cooking time: 15 mins

Ingredients

2 small catfish (about 250g/9 oz each),
  gutted and cleaned, or other freshwater fish
oil, for deep-frying
40g (1½ oz) green mango, peeled, stoned
  and shredded
40g (1½ oz) shallots, thinly sliced
40g (1½ oz) cabbage, shredded
25g (1 oz) roasted peanuts
1 sprig coriander, chopped

For the dressing

3 cloves of garlic, peeled
4 small-medium fresh Thai chillies
2 tbsp fish sauce
2 tbsp lime juice
2 tbsp sugar

1 Preheat the grill to medium-low. Grill the catfish until fully cooked and somewhat dry, about 30 minutes. Remove and allow to cool. Use a fork to remove the skin and coax the flesh from the bones. Discard the bones and skin then chop the flesh finely and set it aside. You should have about 150g (5 oz) of catfish meat.

2 Make the dressing. In a mortar and pestle, pound the garlic until you have a rough paste. Add the chillies, bruising and breaking them into a rough paste. Remove to a small mixing bowl, add the fish sauce, lime juice and sugar, stirring to combine. Adjust the seasoning, if necessary. Remove to a small serving bowl and set aside.

3 Heat the oil in a wok or large pan over a medium-high heat. Squeeze the catfish to remove any moisture. When the oil is hot, add all of the catfish, using a spatula to shape it into a mound so that all the fish sticks together in one unit, and deep-fry until crispy and golden, about 4–6 minutes. Remove from the oil and transfer to a plate lined with kitchen paper to drain.

4 To serve, plate the deep-fried catfish and top with the shredded mango, shallots, cabbage and roasted peanuts. Garnish with the coriander. Serve with the dressing, pouring it over just before eating with freshly cooked rice (see page 264) as part of a Thai meal.

Source //
Executive Sous
Chef Phatsakorn
'Toto' Tatiyaphak
Location //
Celadon restaurant

POMELO SALAD WITH GRILLED CHICKEN & PRAWNS

Yam som oh kai yaang kap kung

From the kitchens of luxury hotel The Sukhothai Bangkok comes this uniquely central Thai-style salad, blending tart citrus fruit, a salty/sweet dressing, and savoury and smoky grilled chicken and prawns.

Yam are often described as salads, but are consumed in a different way than the Western staple. 'Western salads are tart, and are served at the beginning of a meal to encourage the appetite,' explains Phatsakorn 'Toto' Tatiyaphak, of Bangkok restaurant Celadon. 'But *yam* are generally balanced in flavour, and are served along with other dishes, with rice.'

Given that they are consumed more like mains, *yam* tend to be diverse, but generally the primary ingredient is served raw or lightly steamed, and is combined with herbs and a dressing that, especially in Bangkok and central Thailand, balances tart, salty, spicy and sweet flavours.

A classic example of the genre from Bangkok and central Thailand is *yam som oh*, a Thai-style salad based around pomelo, a bowling ball-sized citrus fruit that thrives in the region. A signature dish at Celadon, The Sukhothai Bangkok's Thai restaurant, traditionally, *yam som oh* is served with steamed prawns, but Chef Toto has opted for grilled prawns and chicken, an effort to impart the dish with smoky notes. He also leaves out the dish's chilli, instead emphasising savoury and salty flavours, and has added a bit of crunch in the form of water chestnuts.

'The pomelo mustn't be too sweet,' says the chef of the dish's central ingredient, 'it has to be a bit tart as well.' To counter the sweetness of the fruit, the dish's dressing includes a generous amount of tamarind sauce. This ingredient, from the shelled leguminous fruit common in central Thailand, has a sweet/tart flavour, and can be purchased at Asian grocery stores either as a thick block or a paste. Chef Toto's dressing also includes two types of sugar – white and palm – as well as two types of salty condiments. 'Foreigners don't like the strong taste of fish sauce,' explains the chef, 'so we use salt and soy sauce instead.' ***AB***

Serves 4 as part of a
greater Thai meal

Preparation time: 30 mins
Cooking time: 15 mins

Ingredients

150g (5 oz) grilled chicken breast, shredded
600g (1 lb 5 oz) pomelo segments
50g (2 oz) canned water chestnuts,
*   thinly sliced*
1½ tbsp shredded coconut, toasted
1 tbsp deep-fried crispy garlic (see page 264)
1 tbsp crispy-fried shallots (see page 264)
1½ tbsp roasted peanuts, ground
1½ tbsp dried shrimp, toasted briefly and
*   chopped roughly (optional)*
3 kaffir lime leaves, finely sliced
150g (5 oz) cooked prawns, preferably grilled

For the dressing

2 tbsp tamarind sauce (see page 13)
1 tsp white sugar
1 tbsp palm sugar
1 tbsp light soy sauce
1 tsp salt

Optional garnishes

dried chillies, deep-fried until crispy
deep-fried lotus root slices
anchan flower (Clitoria ternatea)
Asian pennywort
pea shoots

1 In a small bowl, combine the dressing ingredients. Set aside.

2 In a large bowl, combine all the remaining ingredients, except for the prawns. Pour over the dressing and toss. Taste and adjust the seasoning, if necessary. Transfer the salad to a serving plate along with the prawns on the side. Decorate with desired optional garnishes. Serve immediately with freshly cooked rice (see page 264).

Eating fresh raw vegetables

Throughout Thailand, meals are often eaten with pak kiang, *a term that refers to an assortment of local raw fresh herbs and vegetables. Traditionally,* pak kiang *would be anything growing outside one's home such as basil, Thai eggplant, long beans, cucumbers, or winged beans. The vegetables are eaten together with a full Thai meal as a healthy garnish. (In the south of Thailand,* pak kiang *is known as* pak naw.)

แกงคั่วกลิ้ง
โลละ 90฿ ขีดละ 12฿

แกงเผ็ด

แกงเขียวหวาน
โลละ 90฿ ขีดละ 12฿

แกงส้มกลาง
โลละ 90฿ ขีดละ 12฿

แกงเผ็ดใต้
โลละ 80฿ ขีดละ 10฿

แกงส้มใต้
โลละ 80฿ ขีดละ 10฿

น้ำปลา
น้ำส้ม ขวดละ 10฿

CHICKEN GREEN CURRY

Kaeng khiaw waan kai

There's little wonder why green curry, a vibrant intersection of coconut milk, Thai seasonings and a spicy curry paste, is one of the most famous Thai dishes in the world.

Where there's pain, there's also pleasure. At least that's the case according to Saiyuud 'Poo' Diwong at her cooking school in Bangkok. 'When I was young, I used to cry when making curry pastes because Thai people use so much chilli!' explains Poo.

Despite this trauma, Poo stuck with the curry pastes, and decades later, opened the eponymously – and uniquely – titled culinary school, Cooking with Poo by Helping Hands, at her home in Bangkok's Khlong Toei slum. And in what some might consider a cruel twist of fate, one of the most requested recipes at the school is that for kaeng khiaw waan, the chilli-laden dish known abroad as green curry.

Like most central Thai curry dishes, *kaeng khiaw waan* starts with a spicy paste made from pounding a variety of herbs and spices – and chillis – in a granite mortar and pestle. Explains Poo, 'You can make a lot of curry paste in advance and keep it in the freezer.' In addition to a healthy amount of chilli, the paste for green curry also includes the zest of the kaffir lime, a green, knobbly, fragrant citrus fruit most likely unfamiliar to those outside of Southeast Asia.
'We don't use the inside of the kaffir lime as it's too bitter,' says Poo, 'that part is used for shampoo.'

In typical central Thai style, the pungency and spiciness of the chilli paste is tempered by frying in coconut milk. 'Stir-fry the paste in coconut milk until it's fragrant,' explains Poo. 'When the paste smells good, then you add the meat. Coconut milk has fat, so you don't need to use oil.' It is at this point that the curry's other elements and seasonings are added, in this case, additional coconut milk and round, firm Thai aubergines. 'I use half coconut milk and half water,' adds Poo; 'Thai people like crunchy vegetables. If you like them soft, just cook the eggplant a bit longer.' *AB*

Source //
Khun Saiyuud 'Poo' Diwong
Location // Helping Hands
cooking school, Bangkok

CHICKEN GREEN CURRY

Kaeng khiaw waan kai

Serves 2

Preparation time: 45 mins
Cooking time: 30 mins

Ingredients

500ml (18 fl oz) coconut milk
4 kaffir lime leaves, torn
300g (11 oz) skinless chicken breast or
  thigh pieces
6 tbsp fish sauce
1 tbsp sugar
250ml (8 fl oz) water
200g (7 oz) Thai aubergine, halved,
  or 1 regular aubergine, chopped into cubes
small handful Thai basil leaves, to garnish

For the curry paste

1 tsp chopped kaffir lime zest
thumb-sized piece galangal, roughly chopped
5–10 small fresh green Thai chillies, chopped
4 shallots, chopped
3 cloves garlic, chopped
½ small lemongrass stalk, sliced

1 Make the curry paste. In a mortar and pestle, pound the kaffir lime zest and galangal until you have a rough paste. Add the chillies, shallots, garlic and lemongrass and pound until you have a fine paste. Alternatively, whizz them together in a blender or food processor. Set aside.

2 To a large pan over a medium heat, add the coconut milk, the kaffir lime leaves and the curry paste. Simmer for about 5 minutes, stirring to combine, until the mixture is fragrant and slightly reduced. Add the chicken pieces, fish sauce and sugar. Bring to a simmer. Add the water and the aubergine, then simmer for 5–10 minutes until the aubergine is soft and the chicken is cooked.

3 Remove from the heat, add the Thai basil leaves and transfer to a large serving bowl and serve warm with freshly cooked rice (see page 264).

'Making a curry paste is hard work.
But now I have big muscles!'

'Poo' Diwong

RED CURRY WITH PINEAPPLE & PRAWNS

Kaeng khua sapparot kap kung

This classic central Thai curry supplements the richness of coconut milk with prawns while countering it with tart pineapple and tamarind.

According to Chef Vichit Mukura, a native of central Thailand and, for 30 years, Executive Thai Chef at Bangkok's Mandarin Oriental hotel, *kaeng khua* just might be the perfect introduction to central Thai cuisine. 'We encouraged people to order this curry at the Oriental,' explains the chef. 'It's not super spicy, it's pleasantly oily, rich, and mild, and people love that it has three flavours: salty, sweet and sour.'

One in a vast repertoire of central Thai-style curries, *kaeng khua* is similar to the ubiquitous red curry, but is milder in flavour and, in this particular recipe, includes pineapple. 'The pineapple adds a sour and sweet flavour to the dish,' explains Chef Vichit.

Like many other central Thai-style curries, *kaeng khua* is made with coconut milk. This ingredient, a rich, oily liquid extracted from the meat of mature coconuts, not the clear liquid found in green coconuts, is a staple in the central Thai kitchen. 'Coconut milk reduces the spicy flavour of the curry paste,' explains the chef. Cooking with coconut milk can be intimidating for first-timers and involves a stage in which the coconut cream (the thickest liquid obtained from the first pressing) is simmered until it 'cracks', that is, the oil in the cream separates and rises. The ideal curry, 'should have a little bit of oil floating on top,' says Chef Vichit.

Kaeng khua is generally made with seafood, and according to Chef Vichit, large prawns are ideal, as their fat complements the dish's rich taste. Any sort of prawn will do, however, and mussels or even chicken can be used, 'but not beef, it's too strong in flavour,' explains the chef.

And although options may be limited outside of Thailand, Chef Vichit suggests using a pineapple with a good balance of its sweet and sour flavours, and the ripeness of the flesh is less important than the taste: 'There's no need to use a crunchy pineapple, as it gets soft when cooked in the curry anyway.' *AB*

Source //
Khun Vichit Mukura
Location //
Khao restaurant,
Bangkok

RED CURRY WITH PINEAPPLE & PRAWNS

Kaeng khua sapparot kap kung

Preparation time: 15 mins
Cooking time: 30 mins

Ingredients

500ml (18 fl oz) coconut cream
120ml (4 fl oz) hot water
3 tbsp red curry paste
250ml (8 fl oz) coconut milk
3 tbsp fish sauce
2 tbsp palm sugar
220g (8½ oz) tamarind sauce
150g (5 oz) raw king prawns
200g (7 oz) pineapple, peeled and cubed
1 kaffir lime leaf, finely chopped
1 large fresh red Thai chilli, finely sliced

1 In a large pan over a medium heat, bring the coconut cream and hot water to a rolling boil until a thin layer of oil begins to emerge. Add the red curry paste, stirring until fragrant and the oil emerges again. Add the coconut milk, fish sauce, sugar and tamarind and bring to a simmer. Add the prawns and pineapple, simmer until the prawns are pink and firm, then taste and adjust the seasoning if necessary.

2 Remove the pan from the heat, add the kaffir lime and chilli and stir to combine. Serve in a large bowl with freshly cooked rice (see page 264), as part of a Thai meal.

Spoon and fork eating

Traditionally, rice and curry in Thailand was eaten with one's fingers, but nowadays, the most common method is using a spoon and fork combination. The spoon is the principle utensil, while a fork provides support to scoop food onto the spoon. A spoon works better than a fork for eating Thai cuisine because one is able to take a bite of rice mixed with curry, follwed by a spoon of soup, and keep alternating between dishes. Chopsticks in Thailand are typically only used for noodle soup dishes.

EGG & PORK BELLY BRAISED WITH CINNAMON & STAR ANISE

Khai phalo

Hard-boiled eggs, tender pork belly, Thai palm sugar and aromatic dried spices come together in this pleasantly sweet, Chinese-influenced soup.

Thai food isn't always about the spicy stuff. In particular, when it comes to feeding children, there's an entire repertoire of mild, typically Chinese-influenced dishes that Thai parents turn to. One of the most popular examples of this is *khai phalo*, boiled eggs and pork belly in a broth seasoned with Chinese-style spices.

'It's an easy dish to make and eat,' explains one such parent, Amornsri Pattanasitdanggul, of the hearty, fragrant soup. Obviously, kids aren't exactly averse to the dish's inherently sweet flavour. '*Khai phalo* is equal parts sweet and salty,' explains Ann, as she's known. 'I use palm sugar, which gives the dish a caramel flavour and more fragrance. White sugar is too sweet, too sharp.' Yet as she explains, it isn't simply a matter of adding sugar to the broth. 'You have to fry the sugar in the oil so that it becomes caramelised,' says Ann. 'You have to chop the sugar beforehand, otherwise it can stick to the pan and burn.' The mother of two adds, 'I've heard that some people use Coca-Cola in this dish, as it adds a dark colour and a sweet flavour.'

According to Ann, another trick is preparing *khai phalo* in advance. 'The dish gets tastier if you make it a day ahead of time and put it in the refrigerator overnight,' she explains. 'It gets a darker colour and the eggs get pleasantly chewy. I learned this when I was at university, and had lots of leftovers.'

Although hard-boiled eggs and pork belly are the most common ingredients in *phalo*, there are variations. 'If you want to be healthy, you can use tofu instead of pork,' explains Ann. 'You have to use firm tofu, and some people fry it first, to firm it up even more.'

And even though *khai phalo* is a soup, like most Thai soups, it shouldn't be consumed on its own. 'You should eat it with rice,' says Ann, 'and it goes well with a spicy dish because it's slightly sweet.' *AB*

Source //
Khun Amornsri 'Ann' Pattanasitdanggul
Location //
Bangkok

EGG & PORK BELLY BRAISED WITH CINNAMON & STAR ANISE

Khai phalo

**Serves 4 as part of a
greater Thai meal**

Preparation time: 30 mins
Cooking time: 1.5 hrs

Ingredients

3 tbsp oil
200g (7 oz) palm sugar, roughly chopped
*400g (14 oz) pork belly, fat removed, cut
  into 3–4cm (1–1½ inch) long strips*
1½ litres (2½ pints) water
6 hard-boiled eggs
120ml (4 fl oz) light soy sauce
60ml (2 fl oz) dark soy sauce
2–3 cinnamon sticks
2–3 star anise
1 sprig coriander, chopped

For the paste

3–4 coriander roots
3–4 cloves garlic
1 tsp white peppercorns

1 Using a mortar and pestle, pound the coriander roots, garlic and peppercorns until you have a rough paste. Set aside.

2 Place a large, deep saucepan or stock pot over a low heat and add the oil. Once hot, add the paste and stir-fry for 2 minutes until fragrant. Add the sugar, stirring frequently for 2 minutes until combined and slightly caramelised. Add the pork belly and water, increase the heat to medium and bring to a simmer. Add the eggs, soy sauces, cinnamon and star anise, then bring back to a simmer. Reduce the heat to low and allow to simmer, covered, for 1 hour.

3 Remove from heat. Serve in a large bowl, garnished with coriander and accompanied by a bowl of hot steamed rice (see page 264).

*'It's good for kids as it's not too spicy.
It's also a great way to get kids to eat
eggs, which have lots of nutrition.'*

Amornsri Pattanasitdanggul

STIR-FRIED PRAWNS WITH THAI HERBS

Kung phat chaa

An aromatic stir-fry of fresh seafood and seemingly every herb in the Thai larder. It's so flavoursome, Chef Ian recommends serving it alongside – look away, Thailand – something bland.

Source //
Khun Ian Kittichai
Location //
Issaya Siamese Club,
Bangkok

Although the technique of stir-frying in a wok over high heat was likely imported to Thailand from China, by combining it with indigenous ingredients and methods, the Thais have made it their own. *Phat chaa*, a stir-fry of seafood and herbs with origins in central Thailand, is a delicious but relatively little known example of this.

'Phat chaa is a Thai-style stir-fry,' explains Chef Ian Kittichai of Bangkok restaurant, Issaya Siamese Club. 'This means that it's different from the Chinese style, which includes a broth thickened with corn flour.' Like most Thai-style stir-fries, the ingredients in *phat chaa* are loosened with a bit of stock or water rather than a cornstarch slurry, and flavour takes precedence over texture.

Named for the sizzling sound made when the ingredients hit the hot wok, *phat chaa* is a dish associated with fishing villages along the Gulf of Thailand. As such, the dish is made exclusively with fresh seafood. Perhaps the most famous version of *phat chaa* revolves around *hoy lawt*, razor clam-like shellfish from the central Thai seaside city of Samut Songkhram. Versions served elsewhere in central Thailand and Bangkok typically rely on a mixture of seafood, blending thick rings of squid with hearty chunks of fish, prawns and clams.

Of equal importance are the fresh herbs, which in Thai cooking are used to counter the perceived 'fishy' flavours of seafood. An important ingredient in this role here is *krachai*, an aromatic root similar to ginger and galangal, sometimes known in English as fingerroot, lesser ginger or Chinese key. 'It should taste spicy from the *krachai*, chilli and holy basil,' explains Chef Ian of *phat chaa*. In addition to these, garlic and green peppercorns – the fresh version of the ubiquitous western condiment – also make their way into *phat chaa*, making it arguably one of Thailand's most full-flavoured dishes.

Because of its overwhelmingly strong flavours, Chef Ian suggests coupling *phat chaa* with something comparatively low-key. 'It would be good served with a bland, Chinese-style soup, such as one with glass noodles, seaweed or even potatoes,' explains the chef. ***AB***

STIR-FRIED PRAWNS WITH THAI HERBS

Kung phat chaa

*Serves 4 as part of a
    greater Thai meal*

Preparation time: 30 mins
Cooking time: 15 mins

Ingredients

2 tbsp oil
*10–15g small fresh red Thai chillies,
    coarsely chopped*
2 cloves garlic, finely sliced
35g krachai, *peeled and sliced lengthwise*
20g green peppercorns
60ml (2¼ fl oz) chicken stock
16 raw king prawns, shelled
1 tbsp fish sauce
3 tbsp oyster sauce
2 tsp sugar
20g (¾ oz) holy basil leaves
*1 large fresh red Thai chilli, deseeded and
    finely sliced, to garnish*

1 Heat the oil in a wok or large pan over a high heat until smoking. Add the chillies, garlic, *krachai* and peppercorns, stirring to combine until aromatic. Add 30ml of the chicken stock and the prawns, and stir-fry for about 3 minutes until the prawns are almost cooked. Add the fish sauce, oyster sauce, sugar and holy basil, stirring to combine. If the mixture is too dry and it is catching at the bottom of the pan, add the remaining stock.

2 To serve, garnish with the sliced chilli and serve hot with freshly cooked rice (see page 264).

*'If you don't have prawns, the dish can be
made with fish or squid, it depends on what
was caught that day'*

Ian Kittichai

Source //
Khun Nooror Somany Steppe
Location //
Blue Elephant restaurant,
Bangkok

COCONUT & CURRY SPICED PRAWNS

Kung phat phong karii

With origins in China, this dish of prawns wok-fried with egg and a mild curry powder, with the telltale Thai addition of extra chilli heat, has become a local staple.

Many dishes commonly regarded as Thai actually have their origins abroad. In particular, nearly all stir-fried dishes common in Thailand, from fried rice to *phat thai* (Thai-style fried noodles) can be traced back, at least in part, to China. Such is the case with *kung phat phong karii*, an unusual but lauded combination of prawns and curry powder.

Originally thought to have been brought to Thailand by Hokkien Chinese cooks during the 19th or 20th century, the dish, consisting of seafood wok-fried with egg and curry powder, quickly became a staple in Chinese and seafood restaurants across the country. One chef taking the dish beyond *kung phat phong karii's* Chinese origin is Nooror Somany Steppe, owner of Bangkok's Blue Elephant restaurant. 'My recipe is different, it's more Thai as it includes coconut milk and roasted chilli paste,' she explains.

Known in Thai as *nam phrik phao*, roasted chilli paste is a uniquely Thai addition to the original Chinese recipe, and provides the dish with a touch of heat. 'It's made from deep-fried shallots, chilli and garlic that have been ground to paste and cooked again in oil with sugar, fish sauce and tamarind,' explains Chef Nooror, of the condiment. 'I use a bit of the paste when I stir-fry the dish and I also use the oil as a garnish.' *Nam phrik phao* is generally available in tinned form at Asian grocery stores outside of Thailand.

Yet despite the presence of chillies, *kung phat phong karii* remains a predominantly mild dish. 'The curry powder is not hot,' explains the chef. 'The dish should be creamy from the coconut milk and evaporated milk, and fragrant from the curry powder. It should also be a little bit sweet; Thai dishes have to have a balance of flavours. It's normally made with crab, not prawns. You could use scallops or squid instead, but never chicken or beef.' ***AB***

'The dish should be creamy from the coconut milk and evaporated milk, and fragrant from the curry powder. It should also be a little bit sweet; Thai dishes have to have a balance of flavours.'

Nooror Somany Steppe

Serves 4 as part of a greater Thai meal

Preparation time: 30 mins
Cooking time: 15 mins

Ingredients
3 tbsp oil
100g (3½ oz) raw king prawns
½ tbsp light soy sauce
1 tbsp oyster sauce
1 tsp sugar
½ tbsp roasted chilli paste (nam phrik phao)
½ small onion, sliced
1 large fresh red Thai chilli, sliced
1 sprig Chinese celery, cut into 4cm pieces
1 green onion, cut into 4cm lengths

For the egg mixture
1 egg
90ml canned unsweetened evaporated milk
4 tbsp coconut milk
¼ tsp ground turmeric
1 tbsp mild curry powder

For the paste
1 coriander root, roughly chopped
2 cloves garlic
½ tsp ground black pepper

1 In a mortar and pestle, pound the coriander root, garlic and pepper to a rough paste. Set aside.

2 In a small bowl, whisk the egg with the evaporated milk, coconut milk, turmeric and curry powder until well combined. Set aside.

3 Heat the oil in a wok or large pan over a medium heat. Once hot, add the paste, stirring for 2 minutes to combine until fragrant. Add the prawns, stir-frying for just 1 minute until almost cooked. Pour in the egg mixture, soy sauce, oyster sauce, sugar, and the roasted chilli paste, stirring to combine for about 2 minutes until slightly thickened. Mix in the sliced onion, chilli, half of the chopped Chinese celery and half the green onions. Remove from the heat.

4 Pile onto a large serving plate, garnish with remaining Chinese celery and green onion and serve hot, with freshly cooked rice (see page 264).

RICE NOODLES WITH COCONUT SAUCE

Mii kathi

Coconut cream and, well, ketchup come together in this sweet and rich noodle dish with origins in Thailand's royal palace.

Thai cuisine, always blending ingredients new and old, and from across the world, can hardly be accused of being conservative. And a classic example of this is *mii kathi,* a dish of fried rice noodles served with a dressing that includes some unexpected seasonings.

'I think *mii kathi* may originally have come from the Royal Palace,' explains Mallika Thamwattana, owner of Bangkok restaurant Ruen Mallika, 'because it's somewhat sweet and uses rich ingredients from central Thailand.'

The richness in question stems from the addition of coconut cream, a crucial ingredient in the dish's dressing, and a common yet expensive commodity in Bangkok and central Thailand. 'We make our own coconut cream fresh every day, but most street vendors can't afford to use it, and some use whole milk instead,' explains the restaurateur and native of Bangkok.

Another layer of flavour comes, somewhat unusually, from the addition of ketchup. '*Mii kathi* includes ketchup for colour and also to give the dish a sour flavour,' explains Mallika. 'The dish should taste tart followed by sweet and salty. It shouldn't be spicy, but if you like spice, you can add a bit of dried chilli. Otherwise, it doesn't require any additional seasoning.'

Mii kathi revolves around *sen mii,* thin, vermicelli noodles made from rice flour. 'You have to use *sen mii,*' explains Mallika, 'probably to differentiate the dish from *phat thai,* which uses flat rice noodles, and also because they do a good job of absorbing flavours.'

The noodle dish is an example of what the Thais call *ahaan jaan diaw,* or a one-dish meal. 'You don't need to serve it with anything else,' says Mallika, of *mii kathi.* As such, there's a conscious effort to include every flavour in the dish. '*Mii kathi* has no bitter flavour, so we serve it with raw banana blossom, which is astringent. If you can't get that, you can serve it with bean sprouts or green onions.' *AB*

Source //
Khun Mallika
Thamwattana
Location //
Ruen Mallika
restaurant, Bangkok

RICE NOODLES
WITH COCONUT SAUCE
Mii kathi

Serves 2

Preparation time: 1 hr
Cooking time: 15 mins

Ingredients
2 tbsp oil
2 eggs, beaten
150g (5 oz) dried thin vermicelli rice noodles
* (sen mii)*
100ml (3½ fl oz) tomato ketchup
100ml (3½ fl oz) coconut milk
handful garlic chives, chopped
100g (3½ oz) bean sprouts
combination of bitter or astringent vegetables
* or herbs such as banana blossom, Asian*
* pennywort or bean sprouts, to serve*
limes, cut into wedges, to serve

For the coconut sauce
75g (3 oz) shallots, finely sliced
1 onion, finely chopped
380ml (13 fl oz) coconut cream
50g (2 oz) minced prawns
50g (2 oz) minced chicken
50g (2 oz) fermented soybeans, chopped
2½ tbsp sugar
225ml (7½ fl oz) tamarind sauce
* (see page 13)*
2 tbsp fish sauce
5 tbsp tomato ketchup
130g (4½ oz) firm tofu, diced

1 In a wok or medium-sized pan, add the oil and place over a medium heat. When hot, add the eggs, coating the base of the wok to make a thin omelette. When almost cooked, flip the omelette over. Take off the heat and allow to cool. Fold the omelette into thirds and slice it into thin strips. Set aside.

2 Make the coconut dressing. In a saucepan over a low heat, combine the shallots, onion and 80ml (2½ fl oz) of the coconut cream and simmer for 15–20 minutes until fragrant. Increase the heat to medium, add the remaining coconut cream and bring to a simmer. Add the minced prawns and chicken along with the fermented soybeans, stirring to combine. Stir in the sugar, tamarind, fish sauce and ketchup. Bring everything to a simmer. Cook for 20 minutes, then add the tofu, stirring gently to combine and simmer to heat the tofu through. Take the saucepan off the heat and set aside.

3 Meanwhile, soak the rice noodles in a bowl of warm water for 15 minutes. Drain thoroughly and set aside.

4 Place a wok or frying pan over a medium heat, add the ketchup and coconut milk, stirring to combine until reduced slightly. Add the drained rice noodles, stir-frying until the noodles have absorbed the ketchup mixture. Finally, add the garlic chives and bean sprouts, stirring to combine. Remove from the heat.

5 To serve, divide the noodles onto four serving plates, top each with some sliced omelette, the coconut dressing and your chosen optional sides.

HAKKA-STYLE FRIED NOODLES

Phat bamii lueang

Dried squid, soy sauce and thick wheat-and-egg noodles: the unmistakable flavours and textures of China come together in this dish, served in the heart of Bangkok's Chinatown.

The Chinese have had an immense influence on the cuisine of Bangkok and central Thailand. Indeed, many ingredients, dishes and techniques of Chinese origin have become so common and so integrated into the local cuisine, that today they're essentially considered Thai. Yet there are a few dishes, particularly in Bangkok's Chinatown, that to this day remain little changed and still very Chinese.

Such a dish is *phat bamii lueang*, yellow wheat-and-egg noodles stir-fried with an unusual combination of pork and dried squid. 'This dish comes from my father-in-law, who was originally from China,' explains Suthep Chutsiriyingyong, co-owner and cook at Piang Kee, a long-standing restaurant seemingly hidden in a narrow alleyway in Bangkok's Chinatown. 'He was a talented cook who opened this restaurant 40 years ago.'

Like his father-in-law, Suthep is Hakka, an ethnic group that hails from the southeastern part of China. Piang Kee specialises in the unique and, in Thailand, relatively obscure dishes of this group. 'The most common version of fried noodles in Thailand is the Teochew style,' explains Suthep. 'It has carrots, cabbage, mushrooms and tofu. This is the Hakka style of the dish, it includes pork, and the noodles we use are special, they're softer and bigger. The original recipe included shredded *jícama*, but Thai people prefer bean sprouts.'

Yet perhaps *phat bamii lueang's* most noteworthy element is strips of dried squid. Indeed, the unique ingredient lends a salty flavour and a desirably savoury fragrance to several Hakka-style dishes at Piang Kee. 'This recipe is the same as the dish served in China, that's what people who eat here have told us,' says Suthep of Piang Kee's version, which also gets its authentic flavour from Chinese-style seasonings. 'It should be dry in texture, and the dish should taste salty from the light soy sauce and sweet from the dark soy sauce,' explains Suthep, adding, 'but if you don't like sweet, you don't have to use dark soy sauce.' *AB*

Source //
Khun Suthep
Chutsiriyingyong
Location //
Piang Kee restaurant

HAKKA-STYLE FRIED NOODLES
Phat bamii lueang

Serves 4

Preparation time: 15 mins
Cooking time: 15 mins

Ingredients
4 tbsp oil
300g (11 oz) pork fillet, sliced
50g (2 oz) dried squid, soaked in water for a
  few minutes, drained and sliced
800g (1¾ lb) fresh egg noodles
250ml (8 fl oz) pork or fish stock, or water
4 tbsp light soy sauce
2 tbsp dark soy sauce
100g (3½ oz) garlic chives, chopped
200g (7 oz) bean sprouts
ground white pepper
chilli sauce (optional)

1 Add the oil to a wok or a large pan and place over a medium-high heat. When smoking, add the pork and squid, stir-fry for 1 minute until fragrant and almost dry. Add the noodles and half the stock, a little at a time, stirring to combine. Turn the heat down, put on the lid and allow to simmer for about 1 minute. Add the soy sauces and stir-fry for a further minute. If noodles begin to stick or burn, gradually add more stock, a little at a time. Add the garlic chives and bean sprouts, stirring to combine. Taste and adjust the seasoning if necessary.

2 Divide the noodles among serving plates, sprinkle over a dash of white pepper and serve with the chilli sauce, if desired.

'Phat bamii lueang *should be dry in texture, and the dish should taste salty from the light soy sauce and sweet from the dark soy sauce.*'

Suthep Chutsiriyingyong

STIR-FRIED MINCED PORK WITH CHILLIES & HOLY BASIL

Phat kaphrao muu

Minced pork wok-fried with holy basil and no small amount of chilli and garlic: the go-to lunch for the on-the-go Bangkokian.

Given the variety of street food available in Bangkok, it would be nearly impossible to determine what dish is the most popular. But towards the top of the heap would inevitably be *phat kaphrao muu*, a spicy stir-fry of minced pork, chilli, garlic and holy basil.

'Some days I make as many as 50 dishes of *phat kaphrao*,' explains Samruay Choothong, a food cart vendor working in central Bangkok for more than 20 years. 'It sells well because Thai people love strong flavours.'

Indeed, the amount of chillies requested by most diners would shock many outside of Thailand. Yet like many Thai dishes, even the spicy ones, the seasoning of *phat kaphrao* varies from person to person. 'It doesn't have to be spicy – some people don't like spicy,' explains Samruay. 'The dish should be a bit salty and a bit sweet, and dry in texture.'

The chilli heat aside, the dish's predominant flavour is that of holy basil, the eponymous *kaphrao*, an aromatic leafy herb that grows freely in central Thailand. And although it may be hard to find outside of Thailand, resist the urge to substitute *kaphrao* with Thai or Italian basil; there's really no substitute for the intensely fragrant leaf with its spicy little kick.

Another aspect of *phat kaphrao* that undoubtedly appeals to diners is its adaptability. Although pork is the most popular version of the dish, according to Samruay, 'You can make it with seafood – squid or prawns – beef, preserved egg, anything!'

There's really only one constant that concerns *phat kaphrao*, Samruay says: 'It should be served with an egg, a fried egg or omelette. I also serve the dish with a small bowl of soup, sometimes one with pickled vegetables or one with bitter gourd.' And despite its inherent spiciness, *phat kaphrao* always comes with a little bowl of *phrik nam plaa*, thinly sliced fresh chillies in fish sauce, the Thai equivalent of the salt shaker.

Phat kaphrao is perhaps central Thailand's most common example of *ahaan jaan diaw*, a one-dish meal. But it can be included as part of a greater Thai meal. ***AB***

Source //
Khun Samruay Choothong, street vendor
Location //
Thanon Convent

STIR-FRIED MINCED PORK WITH CHILLIES & HOLY BASIL

Phat kaphrao muu

Serves 4

Preparation time: 15 mins
Cooking time: 15 mins

Ingredients
6–9 fresh red Thai chillies, one finely sliced
4 cloves garlic
1 tbsp oil
300g (11 oz) minced pork
1 tbsp oyster sauce
1 tbsp light soy sauce
1 tsp sugar
60ml (2 fl oz) stock or water
75g (3 oz) holy basil leaves
4 fried eggs, to serve (optional)
cooked rice, to serve (optional)

1 In a mortar and pestle, pound the whole chillies and garlic until you have a rough paste. Set aside.

2 Add the oil to a wok or large frying pan and place over a high heat. When smoking, add the pork. Allow to brown for 2–3 minutes, stirring only occasionally. Add the chilli and garlic paste, oyster sauce, soy sauce and sugar, stirring to combine for 2 minutes. Taste, and adjust the seasoning if necessary. If the mixture becomes dry and begins to stick to the pan, add 1–2 tablespoons of stock or water. Add the sliced chilli and holy basil, stirring briefly to combine until the basil has just begun to wilt.

3 Remove from the heat. If serving as part of a Thai meal, remove to a large serving platter and serve hot, with rice. If serving over rice, divide among four plates of cooked rice and top each with a fried egg.

'You can make it with seafood – squid or prawns – beef, preserved egg, anything!'

Samruay Choothong

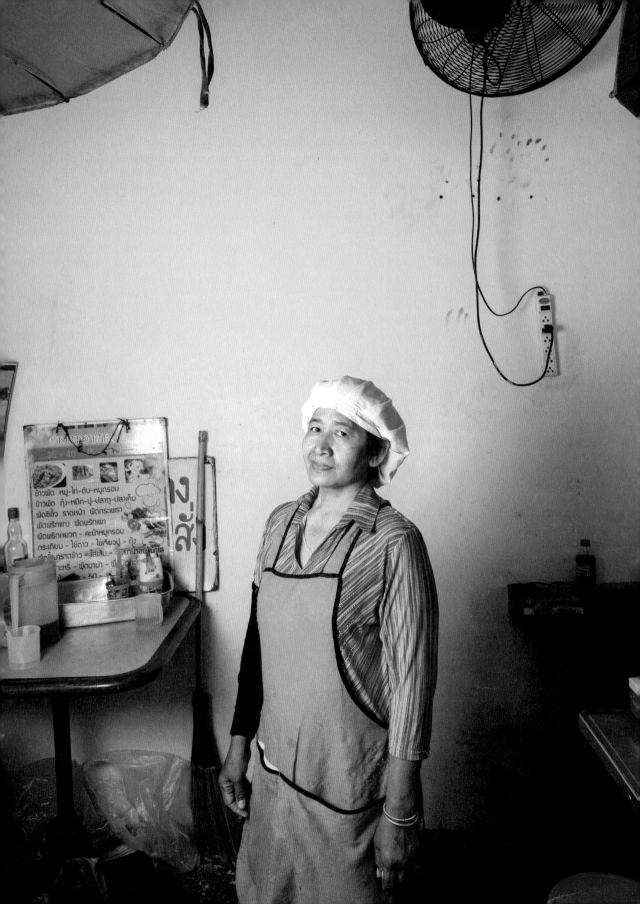

FLASH-FRIED MORNING GLORY

Phat phak bung fai daeng

Crunchy greens flash-fried with garlic, chilli and salty seasonings: a simple yet satisfying combination that's among the most popular street foods in Bangkok.

Morning glory? Water spinach? Water convolvulus? *Ipomoea aquatica? Kangkong? Phak bung?* The overabundance of names hasn't stopped the Thai people – nor visitors to Thailand – from loving this crunchy vegetable.

Morning glory – the current favourite English-language name in Thailand – a hollow green that thrives in wet, swampy areas, is consumed in numerous ways across South-East Asia. In Bangkok and central Thailand, the hands-down preferred method is *fai daeng*, literally 'red fire', a reference to the flames that appear when the vegetable is wok-fried over a high heat along with chillies and garlic. 'It's a Chinese dish that's become Thai,' says Chalatwan Wasasamit, a street stall cook in Bangkok, of the dish. 'Foreigners also like it – it's easy to eat.'

The simple stir-fry is one of the more popular examples of *ahaan jaan diaw*, or one-dish meals, in Thailand. 'People order this dish every day, often served over rice,' explains Pan as she's known, who makes flash-fried morning glory, among other dishes, on her stall in central Bangkok. 'Some people order it with minced pork or crispy pork belly, or served with a fried egg or omelette.' Alternatively, a plate of flash-fried morning glory also functions equally well served along with other dishes, as part of a Thai meal.

Although rarely diverging from a set repertoire of seasonings that includes chilli, garlic, oyster sauce, fermented soybeans, soy sauce and sugar, the dish's flavour is nonetheless subject to personal preference. 'When you order flash-fried morning glory, you need to say how you like it, spicy or sweet,' explains Pan. 'It should be salty and also fragrant from the fermented soybeans. But some people like sweet, and I'll add extra sugar, if they ask.' *AB*

Source //
Khun Chalatwan
'Pan' Wasasamit
Location //
Soi Sala Daeng 2

FLASH-FRIED MORNING GLORY
Phat phak bung fai daeng

Serves 1 as a main or 2 as a starter

Preparation time: 15 mins
Cooking time: 15 mins

Ingredients
½ tbsp oil
200g (7 oz) morning glory, cut into 6cm
  lengths
6 small fresh whole red Thai chillies, smashed
3 cloves garlic, smashed
1 tbsp oyster sauce
½ tbsp fermented soybeans
½ tbsp light soy sauce
½ tbsp sugar
60ml (2 fl oz) stock or water

1 Add the oil to a wok or large pan and place over a high heat. Once smoking, add the morning glory, chillies, garlic, oyster sauce, fermented soybeans, soy sauce and sugar. Stir-fry for 1–2 minutes, adding a trickle of stock or water, a little at a time. Stir-fry for a further 2 minutes or until the morning glory is just cooked and still crunchy.

2 Transfer to a large serving dish and serve immediately.

'There are two unbreakable rules when it comes to phat phak bung fai daeng: *you should eat it hot with rice, and it should be crunchy.'*

'Pan' Wasasamit

CURRIED STIR-FRIED PORK WITH AUBERGINE

Phat phet muu

Taking a form somewhere between a curry and a stir-fry, this classic central Thai dish unites aromatic herbs, bitter pea aubergines, meaty pork and the richness of coconut milk.

F ans of Thai cuisine are undoubtedly familiar with central Thailand's curries, soup-like dishes often including coconut milk and based around a variety of spicy pastes. But few are aware that the pastes used to make Thai curries can also be used in soups that don't include coconut milk, or even in stir-fries that do, such as *phat phet*.

Meaning 'spicy stir-fry', *phat phet* is, admittedly, something of a misnomer. Although the curry paste used to make the dish includes a healthy amount of dried chillies, they are rendered relatively mild by the addition of coconut milk and palm sugar, not to mention a variety of fresh herbs and vegetables, resulting in an almost curry-like stir-fry that is generally more salty and sweet than it is spicy, though it still packs a bit of a wallop.

This recipe for *phat phet* comes from Poj Spa Kar, a restaurant in Bangkok that's said to be among the oldest in the city. 'My husband's grandmother, a former royal palace chef, opened the restaurant 80 years ago,' explains Nathamon Jaidet, the restaurant's current cook.

Although Nathamon's take on *phat phet* may not have explicit palace links, she emphasises, 'We still use the same recipe from 80 years ago, and the flavours are strong, just like in the past.' Those flavours stem from a variety of ingredients that are likely unfamiliar to cooks outside of Thailand including *krachai*, fingerlike, aromatic roots also known as fingerroot or lesser ginger, and green peppercorns, the fresh version of the western tabletop staple. *Phat phet* also uses two types of aubergines common to central Thai cooking: *makhuea proh*, known generally as Thai aubergine, and *makheua phuang*, pea aubergines. The former are the golf-ball sized variety that make sense of the aubergine's other name – eggplant – whereas the latter are green and marble-sized. Thai aubergines soften considerably when cooking, but pea aubergines hold their bite and carry an intensely bitter flavour. ***AB***

Source //
Khun Nathamon Jaidet
Location //
Poj Spa Kar restaurant

CURRIED STIR-FRIED PORK WITH AUBERGINE

Phat phet muu

**Serves 4 as part of a
greater Thai meal**

**Preparation time: 1 hr
Cooking time: 15 mins**

Ingredients

250ml (8 fl oz) coconut milk
150g (5 oz) pork loin, finely sliced
4 kaffir lime leaves, torn
20g (¾oz) krachai (fingerroot), finely sliced
2 large fresh red Thai chillies, finely sliced
20g (¾oz) green peppercorns
120g (4 oz) Thai aubergines, roughly chopped
60g (2 oz) pea aubergines
1 tsp palm sugar
1 tbsp fish sauce
large bunch of Thai basil, leaves picked

For the curry paste

4 small dried Thai chillies
¼ tsp salt
1 lemongrass stalk, outer skin removed,
    interior sliced
3cm (1 inch) piece galangal, sliced
4 cloves garlic, chopped
2 shallots, sliced
1 coriander root, chopped
¼ tsp ground white pepper
½ tbsp shrimp paste
zest of ½ small kaffir lime

1 In a mortar and pestle, pound the chillies and salt to a rough paste. Add the lemongrass and galangal followed by the garlic, shallots and coriander root, pounding everything to a paste. Add the white pepper, shrimp paste and kaffir lime zest and continue to pound until you have a fine paste. Set aside.

2 Add half the coconut milk to a wok or frying pan and set over a medium heat. Add the curry paste. Allow the mixture to reach a simmer, stirring occasionally until slightly reduced. Add the pork, stirring occasionally, until a thin layer of oil has begun to emerge. Increase the heat to medium-high and add the kaffir lime leaves, *krachai*, most of the Thai chilli (reserving a little), peppercorns, both aubergines and the remaining coconut milk. Cook for about 10 minutes, stirring occasionally until the vegetables have softened and the liquid slightly reduced. Add the sugar and fish sauce. Taste and adjust the seasoning if necessary. Add most of the basil leaves, stirring to combine, then remove from the heat.

3 Transfer the pork to a large serving plate and garnish with the chillies and the reserved Thai basil. Serve hot, with rice, as part of a Thai meal.

Source //
Khun Saiyuud
'Poo' Diwong
Location //
Helping Hands
cooking school

THAI FRIED NOODLES WITH PRAWNS & EGG

Phat thai

Spanning salty and sweet, soft and crunchy, this legendary fried noodle dish seems to embrace every beloved flavour and texture in the Thai kitchen.

What is it about *phat thai*, narrow, flat rice noodles fried with egg, prawns and Thai seasonings, that has made it the most popular Thai dish in the world? It might be the fact that *phat thai* unites just about every desirable central Thai flavour, ingredient and texture in one dish.

'*Phat thai* should be sour, sweet and salty, in that order,' explains Saiyuud 'Poo' Diwong of Cooking with Poo by Helping Hands, Bangkok. Traditionally tamarind, a fruit common in central Thailand, is used to provide the dish with its tart flavour, but according to Poo, 'You can use vinegar if you don't have tamarind.' Regardless of the source, this tartness is generally countered by a generous addition of sugar.

Yet breadth of flavour is just one aspect of *phat thai*'s allure. *Phat thai* also incorporates textures including meaty prawns, toothsome rice noodles, tender egg, and crunchy peanuts and bean sprouts. The dish's adaptability also undoubtedly appeals. 'If you don't have prawns, you can use chicken, squid or pork – anything, really,' explains Poo. 'You can also make the dish with glass noodles.'

The only downside with *phat thai*, it seems, is that it can be finicky to make. '*Phat thai* is best to make for one or two people at a time,' explains Poo. 'It's hard to make more than this as the noodles are too sticky.' If the noodles do get unwieldy, 'I use a little bit of oil and a lot of water. If the noodles dry out, I add more water, not oil.'

And because Thai food is as much about appearance as flavour, Poo has yet another tip: 'Cook the egg at the edge of the pan,' she suggests. 'Don't mix it in with the noodles, it looks better this way.'

Phat thai is an example of *ahaan jaan diaw*, a one-dish meal, which means that in Bangkok and central Thailand, it would usually be consumed on its own, not coupled with other dishes as part of a greater Thai meal. **AB**

Serves 4

Preparation time: 30 mins
Cooking time: 15 mins

Ingredients
4 tbsp oil
200g (7 oz) firm tofu, diced
4 shallots, finely sliced
300g (11 oz) raw prawns, shelled
200g (7 oz) dried flat rice noodles
4 tbsp preserved radish, diced
4 tbsp white vinegar
4 tbsp palm sugar
4 tbsp fish sauce
4 tbsp dried shrimp (optional)
4 eggs
small bunch garlic chives, chopped
large handful bean sprouts
4 tbsp crushed roasted peanuts
1 lime, cut into wedges

Optional condiments
chilli powder
fish sauce
sugar

1 Soak the noodles in a large bowl of water for 20 minutes until soft. Drain and set aside.

2 Heat the oil in a wok over a medium-high heat and fry the tofu and shallots, stirring constantly, until fragrant and beginning to colour. Turn up the heat, add the prawns and stir-fry for 2 minutes, until just cooked. Add the rice noodles, preserved radish, vinegar, sugar, fish sauce and dried shrimp (if using), stirring to combine. Add 1 or 2 tablespoons of water a little at a time if the mixture sticks.

3 Push the noodle mixture to one side of the pan and crack in the eggs. Allow them to cook for about 1 minute before mixing everything together. Stir in the garlic chives and bean sprouts. Remove from the heat.

4 Divide the *phat thai* between two serving plates, garnish with crushed peanuts and serve hot with lime wedges and optional condiments of chilli powder, fish sauce and sugar.

'Cook the egg at the edge of the pan, not mixed in with the noodles. It looks better this way.'

Saiyuud 'Poo' Diwong

SWEET, CRISPY PORK RIBS & SALTED SRIRACHA CABBAGE

Sii khrong muu krawp waan

Meaty ribs, Asian spices and a Sriracha-tinged cabbage pickle blend east and west in this unique play on a central Thai staple.

These days Bangkok is an increasingly cosmopolitan city, and not surprisingly the city's food scene has followed suit. One of those helping to take it in an international direction is Danish chef Morten Nielsen, of progressive-minded Bangkok restaurant, Benjarong.

Nielsen's signature dish, and a vivid example of his forward-thinking take on Thai cuisine, is *sii khrong muu krawp waan*, sweet, crispy pork ribs served with salted sriracha cabbage. 'The dish was inspired by *muu waan*,' explains the chef, of central Thai-style sweet pork, 'a dish that's crispy on the outside, soft on the inside, and is sweet, salty and fragrant.'

Yet in what appears to be a deliberate divergence from *muu waan*, which generally relies on cubes of fatty pork, Nielsen has decided to go with that meaty western favourite, ribs. And rather than barbecue them, Nielsen has opted to deep-fry his ribs, serving them with flavourful glaze. 'The ribs should be sweet and a bit salty,' explains Nielsen, 'they should have a soft interior.'

The herbs used to season the glaze, a hand-pounded paste consisting of garlic, coriander root and pepper, show a clear influence of Thai-Chinese cooking ingredients and techniques, although even this is accentuated. 'I add more herbs than usual to provide more fragrance,' explains Nielsen.

Influenced by Thai culinary concepts of balance, Nielsen has chosen to pair his ribs with a unique side dish of salted cabbage spiced with Sriracha. 'It's cabbage similar to the beginning stage of German *sauerkraut*,' explains the chef. 'It looks like *kimchi*, but it's not fermented, and it includes Thai herbs. I include it because the ribs need a complement, something salty and spicy to balance the sweetness. And it has a nice texture, it's crunchy.'

Yet Nielsen seemingly has nothing against omitting this ingredient. 'The ribs could be eaten on their own with a nice glass of beer,' explains the chef. *AB*

Source //
Khun Morten Nielsen
Location //
Benjarong restaurant

SWEET, CRISPY PORK RIBS & SALTED SRIRACHA CABBAGE

Sii khrong muu krawp waan

*Serves 4 as part of a
   greater Thai meal*

*Preparation time: 3 days to salt
   the cabbage + 4 hrs*
Cooking time: 45 mins

Ingredients

500g (18 oz) pork ribs
4 tbsp dark soy sauce
4 tbsp vegetable oil, plus extra for deep-frying
1 tbsp light soy sauce
1 tbsp oyster sauce
2 tbsp fish sauce
240g (8 oz) palm sugar
2 sprig coriander, chopped
*2 tbsp crispy-fried shallots (see page 264)
   (optional)*

For the salted Sriracha cabbage

*500g (1 lb 2 oz) Chinese cabbage,
   leaves separated*
*25g (1 oz) lemongrass stalks, white part only,
   finely sliced*
10g salt
35g (1½ oz) ginger, chopped
10g (½ oz) fresh red Thai chillies, finely sliced
50g (2 oz) spring onions
3 tbsp paprika
1–3 tbsp Sriracha sauce, to taste

For the paste

20g (¾oz) cloves garlic
1 tbsp chopped coriander root
1 tsp white peppercorns

1. Three days beforehand, make the salted sriracha cabbage. Put the cabbage, lemongrass, salt, ginger, chillies, spring onions and paprika in a resealable plastic bag and allow to sit, at room temperature, for three days.

2. On the day of cooking, combine the cabbage mixture with the Sriracha sauce and taste for seasoning. Set aside.

3. Add the pork ribs to a pan of water and just cover with water. Add the soy sauce and simmer the pork for 2–3 hours or until the meat is tender. Remove and drain thoroughly. Heat a pan with enough oil for deep-frying over a high heat. Once very hot, add the ribs and fry for 5 minutes until crispy, then set aside.

4. In a mortar and pestle, pound the garlic and coriander root to a rough paste. Add white pepper and grind to a fine paste. Set aside.

5. Set a large pan or wok over a medium-low heat and add the oil and paste. Stir-fry continuously for 5 minutes, until fragrant. Add the soy sauce, oyster sauce, fish sauce and sugar. Simmer for 3 minutes, stirring to combine, until the sauce is slightly reduced. Increase the heat to medium-high, add the fried ribs and stir until they are well coated. Remove the ribs to a large serving plate and top with the salted Sriracha cabbage. Garnish with coriander and deep-fried shallots (if using) and serve hot with rice (see page 264).

DEEP-FRIED PRAWN PATTIES

Thawt man kung

As a snack or main dish, spicy deep-fried patties of fresh prawns, served with a sweet cucumber-and-peanut dip, tick all the boxes of Thai cuisine.

Although synonymous with powerful flavours and chilli heat, adaptability is an important yet lesser known attribute of Thai cooking. And this openness to playing with ingredients is particularly evident in *thawt man*, deep-fried patties of seafood served with a sweet/spicy cucumber dip, a dish common to central Thailand.

'It's an old recipe that I've adjusted to include prawns instead of freshwater fish,' explains Walit Sitthipan, of Sampran Riverside in Nakhon Pathom, of *thawt man kung*, his take on the dish. 'We live near both the river and the ocean here, so we have access to a lot of resources. I use sea prawns because they have a sweeter flavour.'

Indeed, Nakhon Pathom, located west of Bangkok, is a favourably located province blessed with an abundance of agriculture. Sampran Riverside, the semi-rural resort where Walit is the Director of Food and Beverage, has taken full advantage of this, and is home to an organic farm that supplies much of the restaurant's produce.

The process used to make *thawt man kung* is also subject to adaptation. Although the standard version of the dish is made in a meat grinder or food processor, Walit prefers to combine the ingredients manually, first crushing the prawns with the side of a cleaver then kneading the prawns, egg and curry paste mixture by hand, throwing it against the side of a bowl to break it down. 'I use the same method that Chinese chefs use to make *dim sum*,' explains Walit. 'In doing it by hand, the curry paste mixes better with the prawns.'

Also open to interpretation is the way the dish is consumed. '*Thawt man kung* can be served as an appetiser or a main course,' explains Walit. 'If served as a main, I'd recommend serving it with a stir-fry rather than a curry, because the tastes are too similar.'

Yet one constant is the dish's flavours. According to Walit, '*Thawt man kung* should taste a bit spicy – you can use less curry paste if you don't want it to be too spicy – and it should be served with a slightly sweet dipping sauce.' ***AB***

Source //
Khun Walit Sitthipan
Location //
Sampran Riverside

DEEP-FRIED PRAWN PATTIES

Thawt man kung

***Serves 4 as part of a
greater Thai meal***

Preparation time: 30 mins
Cooking time: 15 mins

Ingredients

300g (11 oz) raw prawns, shelled
1 tsp light soy sauce
1 tsp oyster sauce
1½ tsp red curry paste
3 kaffir lime leaves, finely sliced
*50g (2 oz) long beans or green beans, sliced
   thinly*
1 egg, beaten
oil, for deep-frying

For the cucumber dipping sauce

90g (3¼ oz) cucumber, chopped
25g (1 oz) roasted peanuts, ground
6 tbsp sweet chilli sauce

1 In a small bowl, combine the cucumber, peanuts and sweet chilli sauce. Set aside.

2 Smash the prawns with the side of a cleaver and chop roughly. In a bowl, combine the prawns, soy sauce, oyster sauce, curry paste, kaffir lime leaves, beans and eggs. Use your hands to combine thoroughly, kneading as you go. Tip the mixture onto your hands and throw it back into the bowl – for about 5 minutes.

3 Add the oil to a large frying pan and place over a medium heat. When hot, shape the prawn mixture into patties about 1cm thick and carefully drop them, batches at a time, into the oil. Fry for about 2 minutes or until golden and cooked through. Remove and drain on kitchen paper. Serve hot or at room temperature with the dipping sauce, as an appetiser or as part of a larger meal.

'Thawt man kung *should taste a bit
spicy, but you can use less curry paste if
you don't want it to be too spicy.*'

Walit Sitthipan

CHILLI & COCONUT DIP WITH FRESH HERBS & VEGETABLES

Nam phrik lon

This ancient Thai nam phrik, or chilli-based dip, is mellowed by the addition of coconut cream, herbs and fragrant fruit. Sweet, spicy, salty, it's time to find a snake fruit dealer.

Thai cuisine is home to a vast repertoire of *nam phrik*, spicy, chilli-based dips or relishes. 'Nam phrik is a type of dip served usually with various vegetables,' explains Duangporn 'Bo' Songivsava, of Bangkok restaurant Bo.lan. 'They're found in every region of Thailand, and are an important part of a balanced Thai meal.'

Similar to *nam phrik*, but less common, and primarily associated with Bangkok and central Thailand, is *lon*. 'Normally *lon* has a coconut milk base,' explains Chef Bo. '*Lon* often include preserved ingredients, a mild flavour, and a sweeter front palate. Some *nam phrik* are sour, but most *lon* aren't.'

Even rarer are dishes that blend the two. 'This is an old recipe,' explains Bo of *nam phrik lon*, a dish with the pounded chilli base of a *nam phrik* and the coconut cream broth of a *lon*. 'It's a central Thai dish so it includes ingredients like *ma euk*, coconut cream and *sala*.' *Ma euk* is sometimes known in English as hairy aubergine and *sala* as snake fruit or, following its Indonesian origin, *salak*. Regarding these more obscure ingredients, Bo says, 'If you can't get hairy eggplant, you can use cape gooseberry. But there's no real substitute for snake fruit.'

To those attempting the dish Bo says not to be intimidated by the amount of chillies that go into *nam phrik lon*. 'If making this dish at home, it should have a strong flavour because you're going to eat it with rice.' The balance, he emphasises, is important: 'It should taste spicy at the front of the palate, but also sweet, and salty enough for dipping.'

As with other *nam phrik* and *lon*, the dish should be served with a selection of fresh and blanched vegetables, fruits and herbs. And because *nam phrik lon* is relatively full-flavoured, Bo suggests pairing it with a comparatively subtler dish: 'If serving a spicy *nam phrik*, you should include a mild curry or stir-fry, for balance.' ***AB***

Source //
Khun Duangporn 'Bo'
Songivsava
Location //
Bo.lan restaurant

CHILLI & COCONUT DIP WITH FRESH HERBS & VEGETABLES

Nam phrik lon

**Serves 4 as part of a
greater Thai meal**

Preparation time: 30 mins
Cooking time: 15 mins

Ingredients

60ml (2¼ fl oz) coconut cream
1 tsp palm sugar
1 tbsp fish sauce
½ tsp salt
1 tbsp tamarind sauce (see page 13)
2 slices young ginger, peeled and thinly sliced
*2 slices white turmeric, peeled and thinly
sliced*
1 lime, finely sliced
*25g madan (Garcinia schomburgkiana),
sliced (optional)*
20g salak, peeled and sliced (optional)

For the paste

zest of ½ orange
15g dried shrimp
*3–5 medium-sized prawns, boiled and
chopped*
1 small clove garlic, chopped
2 fresh red Thai chillies
22g ma euk (hairy aubergine, optional)
1 tbsp shrimp paste

Optional sides

white turmeric, peeled and finely sliced
*long beans or green beans, chopped into 4cm
pieces*
cucumber, sliced
okra, par-boiled and halved lengthways
rose apples, finely sliced
star fruit, finely sliced
betel leaves
edible flowers

1 In a mortar and pestle, pound the orange zest, dried shrimp, prawns, garlic, chillies, *ma euk* and shrimp paste until you have a coarse paste. Set aside.

2 In a medium-sized pan over a low heat, bring the coconut cream to a simmer and add the reserved paste. Simmer until fragrant, about 5 minutes. Add the sugar, fish sauce, salt and tamarind, stirring to combine. Add the ginger and if using, white turmeric, lime, *madan* and *salak* and bring to a simmer.

3 Remove from the heat and allow to cool. Serve at room temperature with rice and a selection of fresh vegetables, fruits and herbs.

*'If making this dish at home,
it should have a strong
flavour because you're going
to eat it with rice.'*

'Bo' Songivsava

COCONUT CAKE

Khanom ba bin

The fragrance of coconut, the earthy sweetness of palm sugar and the richness of egg come together in this innovative reinterpretation of a classic central-Thai sweet.

T he Thai word *khanom* is often translated as dessert, but in reality it is closer to a sweet snack, a titbit eaten on its own at any time of day or night. A classic example of the genre in central Thailand is *khanom ba bin*, coin-sized pancakes of batter and coconut meat.

Like other Thai sweet snacks, *khanom ba bin* most likely has its roots in special occasions and ceremonies, but today is ubiquitous, particularly in Ayutthaya, the formal royal capital located just north of Bangkok. '*Khanom ba bin* requires a lot of coconut, so it's only available in the central plains and southern Thailand,' explains Tanongsak 'Dtong' Yordwai, referring to regions of the country where coconuts are grown in abundance. In Ayutthaya, *khanom ba bin* are typically sold from stalls and mobile carts operated predominately by Muslim vendors. 'The version sold on the street is crispy on the outside, brown and nutty,' explains Chef Dtong. 'They're similar to French-style coconut macaroons, but I can't say if they're related.'

At Nahm, the Bangkok fine-dining restaurant where he oversees sweet dishes, Chef Dtong has decided to give *khanom ba bin* a unique twist. 'The version we do here is baked,' explains the chef. 'It's not part of our normal dessert menu; we serve it for special occasions, like a birthday cake.' And in addition to cooking technique and presentation, Chef Dtong's take on *khanom ba bin* is also novel in its ingredients. 'This is a special recipe,' explains the chef, 'on the street, they would use white sugar, fewer eggs, more flour.'

Yet despite having played with the format of the dish, Chef Dtong chooses to maintain *khanom ba bin*'s characteristic consistency and flavour, the result of some unusual ingredients. 'The dish includes arrowroot powder, for a sticky texture,' explains Chef Dtong of the starch derived from cassava, a common ingredient in Thai sweets that should be available at a well-stocked Asian supermarket. ***AB***

Source //
Khun Tanongsak 'Dtong' Yordwai
Location //
Nahm restaurant, Bangkok

COCONUT CAKE
Khanom ba bin

Serves 8

Preparation time: 1.5–2 hrs
Cooking time: 45 mins

Ingredients

120g (4 oz) glutinous rice flour
2 tbsp plain flour
2 tbsp arrowroot powder
pinch of salt
120ml (4 fl oz) water
30ml (1 fl oz) coconut oil
300ml (½ pint) coconut cream, plus
  2 tbsp for drizzling
250g (9 oz) palm sugar
350g (12 oz) finely grated fresh mature
  coconut (about 2 coconuts)
350g (12 oz) shredded young coconut
  (about 2 coconuts)
3 large eggs

1 In a large bowl, combine the flours, arrowroot and salt. Stir in the water and knead together. Cover with cling film and allow to rest for at least an hour.

2 Preheat the oven to 180°C/350°F/gas 4 and grease a 25cm round or rectangular tin with the coconut oil.

3 In a medium saucepan over a low heat, combine 180ml (6 fl oz) of the coconut cream and the sugar and bring to a simmer. Remove from the heat and allow to cool slightly.

4 Stir together the coconut cream mixture and the flour mixture then strain through a sieve into a large bowl. Add both the shredded coconuts, the eggs, one at a time, and the remaining 120ml coconut cream, stirring to combine. Pour the batter into the prepared tin, drizzle with the 2 tablespoons of coconut cream and bake for 45–60 minutes until golden brown. Allow to cool slightly before serving.

'The version sold on the street is crispy on the outside, brown and nutty, similar to a French-style coconut macaroon.'

'Dtong' Yordwai

JASMINE-INFUSED AGAR-AGAR WITH TROPICAL FRUIT SALAD

Khanom dawk mali

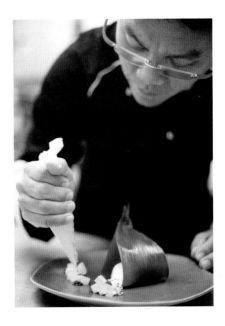

Spain meets Thailand in this jasmine-scented take on flan. Chef Ian Kittichai transforms agar-agar into something as velvety as panna cotta.

'I was living in New York City in the springtime and got fed up with cherry blossoms,' explains Thai Chef Ian Kittichai, when asked about the origin of *khanom dawk mali*, also known as jasmine flan, a dessert served at his Bangkok restaurant, Issaya Siamese Club. 'They were available on menus everywhere, but I couldn't taste them. I thought of replacing them with something from Thailand, and I thought of jasmine.'

Yet Chef Ian's jasmine needed a vehicle, and for this, he yet again turned to Thailand. 'I was influenced by *kathi wun*, Thai-style coconut jelly,' explains the chef and native of Bangkok. 'Coconut jelly is normally kind of crunchy from agar-agar, so I decided to give it a softer texture and add the flavour of jasmine. People are familiar with flan, so I called it that.'

Agar-agar is a flavourless gelling agent derived from seaweed, a common ingredient in Asian desserts. To make his jasmine dessert, Chef Ian couples a relatively small amount of the agent with heavy cream, thus skirting the traditional – and in Asia, desired – toothiness of agar-agar. 'It should be smooth in texture,' explains Chef Ian of his invention, adding, 'it should be creamy and velvety.'

At Issaya Siamese Club, Chef Ian's *khanom dawk mali* is served with exotic-sounding accompaniments such as a rice tuile and jasmine rice ice cream. A significantly more user-friendly version of the dessert pairs the 'flan' with a simple tropical fruit salad, topped, if desired, with crunchy puffed rice and tart passion fruit syrup. 'Serve it with mango – as it's not too overwhelming – jackfruit and dragon fruit,' suggests the chef.

Both the fruit salad and the *khanom dawk mali* should be thoroughly chilled before serving, resulting in a dessert or sweet snack that is ideal for a warm spring or hot summery day. 'It's a great dessert as it's served cool and is refreshing,' adds Chef Ian. **AB**

Source //
Ian Kittichai
Location //
Issaya Siamese Club,
Bangkok

JASMINE-INFUSED AGAR-AGAR WITH TROPICAL FRUIT SALAD

Khanom dawk mali

Serves 4

Preparation time: 2 hrs for setting
   plus 30 mins
Cooking time: 15 mins

Ingredients
1g (0.03 oz) agar-agar powder
275ml (9 fl oz) double cream
40g (1½ oz) sugar
2–3 drops jasmine extract

For the fruit salad
250g diced tropical fresh fruit, such as a mix
   of mango, jackfruit, dragonfruit, mandarin
   orange segments

Optional toppings
puffed rice
passion fruit syrup

1 In a saucepan over a medium heat, bring the agar-agar and cream to the boil. Add the sugar and stir until completely dissolved. Remove from the heat and stir in the jasmine extract.

2 Divide the mixture between four 80ml (2½ fl oz) ramekins. Chill for at least 2 hours or until set.

3 To serve, invert onto a small serving plate and serve with the tropical fruit salad and chosen toppings.

CRISPY COCONUT CUPS

Khanom khrok

Sweet and savoury in flavour, crispy and molten in texture: there's nothing quite like khanom khrok, tiny bowl-like bites of coconut milk and rice batter.

Khanom khrok, literally 'mortar snacks', so called for their distinctly round, bowl-like shape, are one of the more ubiquitous – and beloved – *khanom*, or sweet snacks, in Bangkok and central Thailand.

A combination of rice flour, coconut milk and sugar, the go-to English-language moniker – 'coconut pancakes' – does little to convey the distinctly crispy-on-the-outside, molten-on-the-inside texture of this bite-sized snack. 'The texture should be smooth, and a bit chewy,' explains Piyawadi 'Tam' Jantrupon, of Bangkok's Amita Thai Cooking Class, of *khanom khrok*.

The convenience and ubiquity of the snack mean that they are popular in a variety of situations. 'In the past, *khanom khrok* were served as breakfast,' explains Tam. 'It's a simple snack, one that's easy to eat on the go. I used to eat them on the way to school. The vendors started selling at 6am, and they were never sold past 9am; these days they're served all the time.'

Like other Thai sweets, *khanom khrok* ride a uniquely Thai razor's edge between sweet and savoury. According to Tam, '*Khanom khrok* should be sweet, but not too sweet, and a little bit salty as well.' She adds, 'Many Thai sweets have a bit of salty flavour, for balance.'

Likewise, the standard rice flour and coconut milk batter can be served with sweet or savoury toppings. 'The original version was only topped with green onion,' Tam says. 'Nowadays, there are all kinds of toppings: pumpkin, taro, sweetened egg yolk or water chestnuts.'

Making *khanom khrok* requires a heavy, typically brass or cast-iron pan with small round indentations. According to Tam, 'The pan has to be thick and heavy because *khanom khrok* are made over a low heat, which needs to spread evenly.' *Khanom khrok* pans are sometimes available at Thai grocery stores, otherwise, a Scandinavian or silver dollar pancake pan works. It's even possible to use standard mini-muffin tin covered by a pan lid, or an ovenproof cake-pop mould. **AB**

Source //
Khun Piyawadi 'Tam' Jantrupon
Location //
Amita Thai Cooking Class

CRISPY COCONUT CUPS
Khanom khrok

Serves 4 as a light snack or dessert

Preparation time: 15 mins
Cooking time: 30 mins

For the topping
250ml (8 fl oz) coconut cream
80g (3 oz) sugar
¾ tsp salt

For the base
250ml (8 fl oz) coconut milk
170g glutinous rice flour
1 tbsp sugar
¼ tbsp salt
oil, for greasing

Additional toppings (optional)
fresh corn kernels
green onions, thinly sliced
coriander leaves
kaffir lime leaves, slivered
young coconut meat, shredded

1 In a medium bowl, combine the topping ingredients, stirring until the sugar is fully dissolved. Set aside.

2 In a separate bowl, combine the base ingredients, stirring well until smooth. Set aside.

3 Grease a *khanom khrok* or heavy-based silver dollar pan with oil. Set over a low heat and ladle the base batter into the pan until three-quarters full. Add the topping batter followed by any additional toppings. Cover the pan with a lid and cook for about 5 minutes until crispy and caramelised on the outside, but still soft and runny in the middle. Remove carefully and serve hot as a snack or dessert.

'It's a simple snack, one that's easy to eat on the go. I used to eat them on the way to school.'

'Tam' Jantrupon

COCONUT & MUNG BEAN PUDDING

Maw kaeng thua

Cake-like in form but featuring distinctly Thai ingredients, maw kaeng thua *is one of the more bizarrely wonderful sweet snacks in central Thailand.*

Resembling a cake, but with no flour or leavening; sweet and rich but also savoury; *maw kaeng thua* can be a tough dish to pin down.

'It's something you can find in places where they grow a lot of coconuts and palm sugar,' explains Achareeya 'Nai Noi' Boonyaboosaya, a Bangkok pastry chef, of the central Thai sweet, a rich, almost cake-like combination of palm sugar, eggs, coconut cream and mung beans that's common in the central Thai plains.

Yet despite its distinctly Thai ingredients, *maw kaeng*, a baked dish, seems an unlikely invention, as few Thais own ovens. 'In the past, people cooked it on a stovetop in a clay pot – that's where the name of the dish comes from,' explains Nai Noi of the eponymous *maw kaeng*, Thai for 'curry pot'. She explains that during this process, Thais would cover the clay plot with a metal lid piled with hot coals, an effort to 'bake' the top of the dish. To recreate this, Nai Noi suggests baking the *maw kaeng* on the top rack of an oven so it browns nicely.

Maw kaeng's rich base ingredients are standard, but there are numerous additions and variations on the dish. According to Nai Noi: '*Maw kaeng* can be made with taro – that's a popular one – pumpkin or soybean. I've seen it with lotus seeds on top, and chestnuts would also be good.'

'It should be rich, but not too sweet,' she explains. 'Thai people eat *maw kaeng* as a snack, generally in the afternoon, not really after a meal – it's too heavy for that. It should have a little savoury flavour – the fried shallot plays a big role in that. And this version has beans, so it shouldn't be too eggy.'

The pastry chef embraces the dish's go-your-own-way ethic: 'If you can't get palm sugar, you can use white sugar, but it won't be as fragrant. I've also made it with vanilla extract – it was different!' *AB*

Source //
Khun Achareeya 'Nai Noi'
Boonyaboosaya, pastry chef
Location // Bangkok

COCONUT & MUNG BEAN PUDDING

Maw kaeng thua

Serves 4 as a light snack or dessert

Preparation time: 3 hrs
Cooking time: 1 hr

Ingredients

85g (3 oz) dried mung beans
3–4 tbsp vegetable oil, plus extra
   for greasing
2 shallots, finely sliced
100g (3½ fl oz) palm sugar or white sugar
3 eggs
pinch of salt
2 pandan leaves
120ml (4 fl oz) coconut milk

1 Soak the mung beans in a bowl of water for 3 hours or overnight. Rinse well and cook in a steamer (or rice cooker) for about 30–35 minutes or until soft. Set aside and allow to cool.

2 Preheat the oven to 160°C/325°F/gas 3 and grease a 20cm (7 inch) round cake tin or four small ramekins.

3 Place a small frying pan over a low heat, add the oil and fry the shallots until golden brown and crisp. Drain the shallots, reserving 1 tablespoon of the oil, and set aside.

4 In a medium bowl, combine the sugar, eggs, salt and pandan leaves. Mix ingredients by hand, squeezing the leaves to extract the pandan aromas. Discard the leaves and strain the mixture through a sieve into another bowl. Whisk (by hand or with a stand mixer) the mixture until pale and frothy. Set aside.

5 Put the mung beans into a blender or food processor with the coconut milk and the reserved tablespoon of oil. Blend to a smooth consistency. Add this mixture to the egg mixture and stir to combine. Pour the batter into the prepared tin or ramekins and bake for 25 minutes. Remove from the oven, sprinkle over the crispy-fried shallots and bake for another 5 minutes until firm and golden. Allow to cool on a wire rack and serve at room temperature as a snack or dessert.

Source //
Khun Duangporn 'Bo'
Songivsava
Location //
Bo.lan restaurant

TAPIOCA DUMPLINGS IN COCONUT CREAM

'Pu ngat

Tender tapioca dumplings and fruit swim together in a salty-sweet coconut broth for this obscure yet uniquely central Thai-style dessert.

It's not an exaggeration to say that *pu ngat* is something of a mystery dish. 'The name doesn't mean anything in Thai, and nobody knows where it came from; I got this recipe from an old cookbook,' explains Duangporn 'Bo' Songivsava, of Bangkok restaurant Bo.lan, of the obscure sweet.

What is clear, at least according to Bo, is that the dish, a mixture of tapioca dumplings, bananas and potatoes served in sweetened coconut cream, is a variation on a type of Thai dessert known as *buat*. 'To make *buat*, you take some sort of fruit or vegetable that has lots of carbohydrates and simmer it in coconut cream,' explains the chef. 'It's a super-common type of dessert in central Thailand, and can be made with pumpkin, banana, taro or sweet potato.'

Traditionally, the recipe for *buat* involves soaking the starchy ingredients in a slaked lime solution. Also known in English as acidulated limewater or limestone solution, and in Thai as *nam poon sai*, slaked lime has nothing to do with the citrus fruit, but rather is a mixture of calcium hydroxide and turmeric that has been dissolved in water. 'The slaked lime solution helps fruit hold together while it's being simmered,' says Bo of the unique ingredient, which is also used in Thai-style batters to provide a crispy texture when deep-frying.

Another unique technique, also employed at Bo.lan, is to smoke the finished *pu ngat* with a candle made from scented woods, essential oils and even civet musk. 'We do this to impart scents and make the aroma more diverse,' explains Bo. 'Thai food is often about aroma, not just flavour, people often forget about this!'

'It strikes me as a very Thai dessert,' says Bo. 'It doesn't include wheat flour or eggs, and even the technique is very simple. And like all Thai desserts, it has a salty element. It's important to balance the salty and sweet.' ***AB***

Serves 4

Preparation time: 1 hr
Cooking time: 30 mins

Ingredients
60g (2¼ oz) banana, cut into 4cm pieces
60g (2¼ oz) taro, cut into 4cm pieces
60g (2¼ oz) sweet potato, cut into 4cm pieces

1 litre (1¾ pints) slaked lime solution
  (optional)

120g (4 oz) tapioca flour
3 tbsp water, coloured green with a few drops
  pandan essence or food colouring
250ml (8 fl oz) coconut cream
60g (2½ oz) sugar
1 tsp salt
1 pandan leaf, tied in a knot

1 Thai scented candle (optional)

1 In a large bowl, combine the banana, taro, sweet potato and, if using, the slaked lime solution. Leave to sit for 15 minutes. Strain and set aside.

2 In a medium-sized bowl, combine the tapioca flour and the water to form a dough. Roll the dough into pencil-thick logs and cut into 4cm long pieces. Set aside.

3 In a large saucepan, cover the banana, taro and sweet potato with plenty of water and bring to a simmer. Cook for 20 minutes until soft. Use a slotted spoon to remove the cooked fruit and vegetables from the water and set aside. Add the tapioca dumplings, in batches, to the simmering water and cook until they float to the surface. Transfer to a bowl of iced water. Drain and set aside.

4 In a separate saucepan over a medium heat, combine the coconut cream, sugar, salt and pandan leaf (if using). Stir for 2 minutes to dissolve the sugar and salt, then bring to a simmer. Add the banana, taro, sweet potato and tapioca dumplings. Simmer again, take off the heat, discard pandan leaf (if using), and set aside until mixture has reached room temperature. If using a Thai scented candle, light the candle, place it and the *pu ngat* under a large bowl (which will extinguish the candle) and leave to infuse for 30 minutes. Serve at room temperature divided into bowls.

'Thai food is often about
aroma, not just flavour'

'Bo' Songivsava

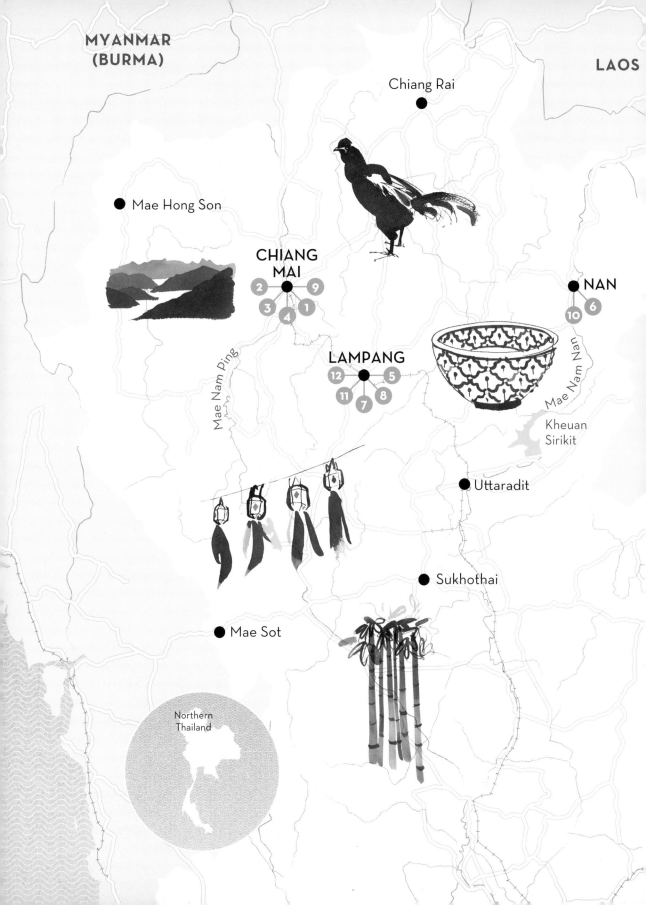

MYANMAR
(BURMA)

LAOS

Chiang Rai

Mae Hong Son

CHIANG
MAI
2   9
3   1
4

NAN
6
10

LAMPANG
12   5
11   8
7

Mae Nam Ping

Mae Nam Nan

Kheuan
Sirikit

Uttaradit

Sukhothai

Mae Sot

Northern
Thailand

NORTHERN THAILAND

Mild, seasonal dishes with ancient roots

NORTHERN-STYLE SPICY CHICKEN SOUP

Yam jin kai

This northern take on a classic Thai soup forgoes the usual tart lime juice and replaces it with an emphasis on savoury flavours and a unique mixture of dried spices.

Tom yam, a central Thai, spicy/sour soup typically revolving around fresh herbs, spicy chillies, lime juice and shrimp, is a dish well known beyond Thailand's borders. But few, even within Thailand, are familiar with *yam jin kai*, the northern Thai variant.

'*Yam jin kai* includes lots of dried spices, making it more fragrant than the central Thai version,' explains Amara 'Aum' Chaiprasert, Sous Chef at Le Grand Lanna, the Thai restaurant at the Dhara Dhevi Chiang Mai. The spices Chef Aum is referring to are those used to flavour northern Thai-style *laap*, a unique blend of as many as 10 ingredients that range from coriander seed to the more obscure prickly ash (for details on this, see page 133).

Also veering from the central Thai version of the dish is *yam jin kai*'s emphasis on salty and savoury flavours. 'Northern people don't like sweet, so this dish doesn't have any sugar,' explains the native of Chiang Mai.

Yet like central Thailand's beloved *tom yam*, fresh herbs play a huge role in seasoning *yam jin kai*, forming the basis of the soup's stock. Chef Aum's take on the dish sees the fragrant but coarse herbs used to flavour the broth – galangal, lemongrass and kaffir lime leaves – removed before serving. They can be left in, if desired, but much like bay leaf in Western cooking, they aren't meant to be eaten.

Fresh herbs also form the soup's garnish. '*Yam jin kai* includes Vietnamese mint and sawtooth coriander,' explains Chef Aum. 'If you can't get Vietnamese mint, you can use regular mint, and if you can't get sawtooth coriander, you can use regular coriander.'

Although there are variations on *yam jin kai*'s main ingredient, which can range from frogs to freshwater fish, according to Aum. 'Usually we use chicken. It never includes seafood, as we don't have much of that up north!' *AB*

Source //
Amara 'Aum' Chaiprasert
Location //
Le Grand Lanna
restaurant, Chiang Mai

NORTHERN-STYLE SPICY CHICKEN SOUP

Yam jin kai

Serves 1–2

Preparation time: 15 mins
Cooking time: 30 mins

Ingredients

700ml (1½ pint) chicken stock or water
thumb-sized piece galangal (10g/¼ oz),
*   peeled and sliced*
1 lemongrass stalk, outer leaves peeled,
*   roughly sliced*
2 kaffir lime leaves, torn
100g (3½ oz) chicken breast fillet
1 tbsp shrimp paste
1 tsp fish sauce
1 tbsp Northern Thai laap *spices (see*
*   Northern Thai Minced Pork Salad, page*
*   133), ground*
1 sprig Vietnamese mint or regular mint,
*   finely chopped*
1 spring onion, finely chopped
1 sprig sawtooth coriander, finely chopped
cooked sticky rice, to serve

1 In a large pan over a high heat, bring the stock or water to the boil. Reduce the heat to medium-low, add the galangal, lemongrass and kaffir lime leaves and simmer for 30 seconds. Add the chicken, simmer for 10 minutes until cooked then remove and set aside to cool. Use a slotted spoon to remove and discard the galangal, lemongrass, and kaffir lime leaves from the stock. Leave the stock in the pan.

2 When cool enough to handle, shred the chicken. Set aside.

3 Bring the stock back to the boil. Add the shrimp paste, fish sauce and Northern Thai *laap* spices, stirring to combine, then reduce the heat to low. Taste and adjust the seasoning if necessary. Add the shredded chicken and bring to a simmer. Remove from the heat, add the mint, spring onion and sawtooth coriander. Remove to a large serving bowl and serve immediately with sticky rice (see page 264).

Sticky rice

In the northeastern and northern regions of Thailand, sticky rice, better known as khao neow, *is the staple. Typically, a family-sized batch of sticky rice is steamed in the morning, then transferred to a* kratib khao neow, *a large circular basket with a lid, which keeps it moist and fluffy throughout the day. At mealtimes, a small bite of sticky rice, about the size of an olive, is formed into a ball and eaten directly, or dipped into the dressing or sauce of a dish to give it flavour.*

Source //
Amara 'Aum' Chaiprasert
Location //
Le Grand Lanna restaurant,
Chiang Mai

SOUR PORK STIR-FRIED WITH EGG

Jim som khua kap khai

Tart fermented pork and rich eggs cross paths in this uniquely northern stir-fry.

Early fusion? Amara 'Aum' Chaiprasert, Sous Chef at Le Grand Lanna, the Thai restaurant at the Dhara Dhevi Chiang Mai, seems to think so. 'Sour pork is a northern ingredient, but frying is a central Thai technique, one with Chinese origins,' she explains. These disparate ingredients and techniques come together in *jim som khua kap khai*, sour pork stir-fried with egg, a dish common across northern Thailand.

The sour pork in question is *jin som*, a mixture of pork, rice and seasonings left to ferment in banana-leaf wrappers or earthenware pots for three days. 'The *jin som* gives the dish a tart flavour,' says Chef Aum, explaining that, *jin som*, literally 'sour meat', is one of the most beloved ingredients in northern Thailand, whether eaten on its own – raw or cooked – or added to soups, salads and stir-fries. It is generally available at Asian food stores outside of Thailand, where it goes by the more common central Thai name *naem*.

Here, *jin som*'s assertive tartness is foiled by the addition of rich eggs. 'Our recipe uses three types: raw, preserved and boiled,' explains the chef. 'This gives diners the chance to try several types of Thai eggs.' Prepared seasonings, herbs and spices also play a role in tempering the sour flavour of *jin som*. The seasonings are pretty standard for a Thai-style stir-fried dish: sugar, soy sauce, oyster sauce and fish sauce. She adds, 'We use fresh garlic, because it's fragrant. Some people use pickled garlic, but that adds a lot of sweetness. We also add white pepper to give the dish a spicy flavour that foreigners can tolerate; northern Thais would probably use fresh chillies instead.' ***AB***

'Our recipe uses three types: raw, preserved and boiled. This gives diners the chance to try several types of Thai eggs.'

'Aum' Chaiprasert

Serves 4 as part of a
greater Thai meal

Preparation time: 15 mins
Cooking time: 15 mins

Ingredients
2 tbsp vegetable oil
2 cloves garlic, finely chopped
3 fresh bird's eye chillies (optional), chopped
100g (3½ oz) fermented pork (jin som),
*   roughly chopped*
1 egg
1 tsp sugar
1 tsp light soy sauce
1 tsp fish sauce
1 tsp oyster sauce
1 large fresh red or green Thai chilli, sliced
1 spring onion, sliced
½ hard-boiled preserved egg, quartered
½ hard-boiled salted egg, quartered
½ hard-boiled egg, quartered
pinch of ground white pepper

1 Heat the oil in a wok or large frying pan over a medium heat. Add the garlic and bird's eye chillies (if using) and stir-fry briefly to combine. Add the fermented pork and crack in the egg, stirring until it is just cooked. Add the sugar, soy sauce, fish sauce and oyster sauce, stirring to combine.

2 Increase the heat to high, add the large Thai chilli, spring onion, preserved egg, salted egg and hard-boiled egg, stirring briefly to combine. Taste and adjust the seasoning, if necessary.

3 Remove to a plate, sprinkle over the white pepper. Serve hot with freshly cooked rice (see page 264).

CHIANG MAI PORK CURRY

Kaeng hang lay

Richness and balance are the key terms in describing this classic northern Thai curry of pork belly, a mild dried spice mixture, ginger and tamarind.

A standard at traditional northern Thai festivals and Chiang Mai's tourist restaurants alike, *kaeng hang lay*, a rich curry that blends pork belly, dried spices, fresh ginger and garlic, is among the most beloved dishes in the northern Thai repertoire. Yet it may in fact be an import. 'I think *kaeng hang lay* is a Burmese recipe,' explains Pongsak Siriphan at Tamarind Village, Chiang Mai, the home of Ruen Tamarind restaurant, 'as it includes a lot of dried spices, unusual for a Thai dish.'

The spices in question take the form of a blend known as *phong hang lay*. 'In the past, there was no *phong hang lay* for sale, people made it themselves,' explains Pongsak of the mixture that can include more than 10 different spices. He adds, 'If you can't get *phong hang lay*, you can use garam masala. It's almost the same.'

Yet dried spices are just one element of *kaeng hang lay*, a dish that features just about every Thai flavour. 'It should taste a bit sour and a bit sweet because it has tamarind pulp and sugar,' says Pongsak. 'It shouldn't include fish sauce, but rather salt.'

Like many culinary standards, *kaeng hang lay* is subject to significant variation. 'There are several different recipes for the dish in northern Thailand,' explains Pongsak. 'Our recipe uses pork collar as well as pork belly, otherwise it would be too fatty. Some people use pickled garlic, but that makes the dish sweeter. And if you want, you can make it with red curry paste, the ingredients are almost the same.'

'*Kaeng hang lay* may look intimidating, but it's actually an easy dish to make,' adds Pongsak. Yet, as he explains, it is a dish that benefits from patience. 'We marinate the pork first so the flavour gets into the meat. Some people marinate it overnight, which makes it even more delicious.' According to Pongsak, it's also important not to rush the cooking: '*Kaeng hang lay* is an example of slow cooking. It should simmer until it's thick and rich; it's a curry, not a soup.' *AB*

Source //
Pongsak Siriphan
Location //
Ruen Tamarind, Chiang Mai

CHIANG MAI PORK CURRY

Kaeng hang lay

Serves 4 as part of a
  greater Thai meal

Preparation time: 1 hr
Cooking time: 1 hr

Ingredients

500g (1 lb 2 oz) pork belly, cut into about
  4cm (2 inch) pieces
1 tbsp hang lay or ground garam masala
3 tbsp palm sugar
1 litre (1¾ pints) water
1 tbsp dark soy sauce
2 tbsp tamarind sauce (see page 13)
6–8 cloves garlic
4–6 shallots, halved
3 tbsp chopped ginger, to garnish

For the curry paste

5–8 large dried Thai chillies
1cm piece galangal, finely sliced
1 lemongrass stalk, outer leaves removed,
  sliced
4 cloves garlic, finely chopped
1 tsp shrimp paste
3 shallots, finely sliced

1 Using a mortar and pestle or food processor, grind the curry paste ingredients, one at a time, until you have a fine paste. Set aside.

2 In a large mixing bowl, combine the curry paste, pork belly and *hang lay* or masala. Leave to marinate at room temperature for at least 30 minutes or overnight in a refrigerator.

3 Heat a wok or large pan over a medium heat. Add the marinated pork and water. Bring to the boil then reduce heat to a low simmer. Add the sugar, soy sauce and tamarind, stirring to combine. Simmer for 20 minutes, taste and adjust the seasoning if necessary. Stir in the garlic and shallots, and simmer for a further 10 minutes. Transfer to a large serving bowl and garnish with ginger. Serve warm or at room temperature with sticky rice (see page 264). Any leftover curry can be used to make Stir-fried Curry Noodles on page 149.

NORTHERN-STYLE MINCED PORK SALAD

Laap muu khua

Not your local Thai joint's laap; *this 'salad' of minced pork, with origins in northern Thailand, blends exotic dried spices, salty/savoury flavours and fresh herbs.*

Laap (or *larp* or *larb*), a tart, spicy, herbal salad of minced meat from northeastern Thailand, has become a standard both domestically and abroad. But the northern version of the dish is an entirely different beast altogether. 'Northern Thai-style *laap* uses up to 10 dried spices,' explains Nitipong Moong Ngern of Small House Thai Cooking School, Chiang Mai.

While the more common northeastern version of the dish gets its kick from lime juice, fresh chillies and herbs, the northern version takes an earthier route, relying on spices not seen elsewhere in Thai cooking, most notably, *makhwaen*. Also known as prickly ash, *makhwaen* is a spice known for its sensation as much as for its flavour. '*Makhwaen* makes your mouth a bit numb,' says Arm, as he's known. 'It's quite strong, somewhat like Sichuan pepper.' Other spices commonly used in northern Thai-style *laap* include star anise, cinnamon, coriander and the more exotic long pepper.

The other important consideration is the meat. 'Usually *laap* is made with beef or pork,' explains Arm, 'There's also chicken and buffalo *laap*, but those are hard to find. Actually, you can make *laap* with just about any meat; people in remote areas make it with monitor lizard or deer.' Regardless of the protein used, texture is key. Arm is strict on this: 'Store-bought ground pork just isn't fine enough. You have to chop it by hand to get the right texture.'

And it doesn't stop at exotic minced meats. In northern Thailand, *laap* usually includes offal and sometimes, blood. And there's also the question of whether to cook the dish, as it can be served raw or cooked. Arm's reasoning for preferring the latter seems sound: 'The raw flavour is pretty strong, and I'm scared of parasites!'

Regardless of its ingredients or how it's served, to balance its inherent meatiness, *laap* is always served alongside a heaped platter of vegetables and herbs. 'If you just eat meat, it's too heavy. *Laap* should be eaten with cabbage, eggplants, long beans and fresh herbs,' explains Arm. 'It should also be eaten with sticky rice.' *AB*

Chef //
Nitipong 'Arm' Moong Ngern
Location //
Small House Thai Cooking
School, Chiang Mai

NORTHERN-STYLE MINCED PORK SALAD

Laap muu khua

**Serves 4 as part of a
greater Thai meal**

Preparation time: 1 hr
Cooking time: 15 mins

Ingredients

4 tbsp oil
1 clove garlic, finely chopped
200g (7 oz) minced pork
100g (3½ oz) pork offal (liver and kidney),
   finely sliced
¼ tsp salt
1 sprig mint, leaves chopped
1 spring onion, chopped
bunch coriander chopped
1 tbsp crispy-fried garlic (see page 264)

For the spice mixture

¼ tsp dried chilli
½ tsp coriander seed
¼ tsp makhwaen (Zanthoxylum limonella,
   also known as prickly ash)
¼ tsp long pepper
¼ tsp cloves
¼ tsp star anise
¼ tsp cinnamon
¼ tsp Siamese cardamom
¼ tsp black pepper
¼ tsp salt

Optional sides

Napa cabbage
assorted lettuce leaves
Thai aubergines, sliced
long beans or green beans
cucumber, sliced
assorted leaves of mint, coriander
   and/or Thai or Vietnamese basil

1. Place a small pan over a low heat and dry-roast the spice mixture ingredients, except the salt, until darker and fragrant. When cool, grind in a mortar and pestle or coffee grinder until you have a fine powder. Stir in the salt and set aside.

2. Add the oil to a wok or large pan and place over a medium heat. When hot, add the chopped garlic, pork and the spice mixture and stir-fry until the pork is cooked. Add the salt, taste and adjust the seasoning if necessary. Remove from the heat, add half the mint, spring onion and coriander, stirring to combine.

3. Transfer to a large serving plate and sprinkle over the remaining fresh herbs and the crispy-fried garlic. Serve the *laap* hot or at room temperature with sticky rice (see page 264) and a selection of fresh vegetables.

'Store-bought ground pork just isn't fine enough. You have to chop it by hand to get the right texture.'

'Arm' Moong Ngern

PORK, VEGETABLE & MUSHROOM SOUP

Kaeng khae muu

Khun Junob Tongdee makes and sells soup at Kao Jao Market in Lampang. Every ingredient in her kaeng khae, *a nourishing vegetable and mushroom soup, comes from the market.*

K aeng khae is a popular soup prepared with local, and sometimes wild, vegetables and mushrooms, simmered with a choice of meat. Chunky and chock-full, it's perhaps better considered a vegetable stew or curry. It's delicious, but people in northern Thailand also eat *kaeng khae* because it's considered a dish with medicinal value.

Khun Junob Tongdee makes and sells soups at Kao Jao Market. The market, located just down the tracks from Lampang Railway Station, has existed for over 100 years, and is well known for preserving traditional northern Thai ingredients and dishes. The market's vendors sell wild herbs and mushrooms from the forest. 'All the dishes I make use local vegetables, herbs and mushrooms, which are easy to find here,' Junob explains.

Junob is hardly new to cooking, or to the market environment, her mother previously having the same stall. 'I learned all my recipes from her,' she says. Starting the day at around 3am each morning, Junob begins washing and chopping all the fresh ingredients she needs to make five to six different soups. She does the cooking in a small outdoor kitchen in the main part of the market, and by around 6am, when she's finished preparing, she sets up a table on the street-facing portion of the market and lines up each dish in a shiny metal bowl. By the time she's ready, customers are already waiting. 'Many are repeat customers from the neighbourhood who come to buy food every day,' Junob says.

'Traditionally, we eat *kaeng khae* with sticky rice,' she explains, 'but nowadays some people eat it with jasmine rice too.' Her *kaeng khae muu*, a version made with pork, is prepared hot and fresh, with a delectable aroma of lemongrass and galangal, and just a subtle hint of fermented fish sauce. The local lentinus mushrooms she likes to use have a tough texture and offer a chewy element to the soup. But the true emphasis, for any bowl of *kaeng khae*, is on the vegetables, which are never overcooked, but crisp and naturally sweet, with a taste of the forest in each bite. *MW*

Chef //
Khun Junob Tongdee
Location //
Kao Jao Market, Lampang

PORK, VEGETABLE & MUSHROOM SOUP

Kaeng khae muu

Serves 2

Preparation time: 40 mins
Cooking time: 10 mins

Ingredients
600ml (1 pint) water
200g (7 oz) lean pork, cut into
  bite-sized pieces
200g (7 oz) choi sum or pak choi, sliced
5 long beans or handful green beans,
  roughly chopped
100g (3½ oz) mangetout
100g (3½ oz) mixed wild mushrooms or
  button mushrooms
2 fresh red Thai chillies, crushed
3 kaffir lime leaves, torn
1 tbsp fermented fish sauce (pla ra, optional)

For the curry paste
2–3 fresh red or green Thai chillies
10 cloves garlic, chopped
5 shallots, chopped
2 lemongrass stalks, outer skin and top stem
  removed, finely sliced
thumb-sized piece galangal, finely sliced
½ tsp salt
1 tsp shrimp paste

1 In a mortar and pestle, pound the chillies, garlic, shallots, lemongrass, galangal, and salt for about 20 minutes until you have a coarse paste. Add the shrimp paste and pound for 5 more minutes until fully mixed.

2 Add 100ml (3½ fl oz) of the water to a medium-sized pan and bring to the boil. Add the curry paste and stir for about 3 minutes, making sure it fully dissolves and the aromas begin to release.

3 Add the pork and bring the soup to the boil again. Cook for about 5 minutes until the pork is fully done. Add a remaining 500ml (1 pint) of water and bring to a simmer on low heat for 5 more minutes.

4 Add the crushed chillies and kaffir lime leaves followed by the vegetables and mushrooms. Simmer for 2–3 minutes – the vegetables should be just cooked but still have some crunch. Turn off the heat, then finally add the fermented fish sauce (optional), give it a final stir, and serve immediately.

ROASTED CATFISH IN BANANA LEAF

Aeb pla duk

It's purely out of love that Khun Rabiab Kamsang cooks and sells aeb, *a northern Thai mixture of meat (often fish) and spices roasted in a banana leaf parcel.*

K hun Rabiab Kamsang is known throughout Nan for her *aeb*. It's a northern Thai food, often prepared with fish, marinated in spices, wrapped in a banana leaf parcel, and roasted over fire. In the north of Thailand *aeb* is commonly found at street food stalls and considered a great takeaway dish to eat on the go. '*Aeb* is an entire meal all in one simple and delicious parcel,' says Rabiab, 'all you need with it is sticky rice.'

Rabiab, or Pa Nun as she is known, does all the cooking at home. In the morning she sells her stock to third-party vendors who resell the *aeb* at markets around town. In the evening, Rabiab makes another batch, which she sells at the market herself. 'People in Nan know which *aeb* is mine because of the way I wrap and fasten the banana leaves,' she explains. Pa Nun's *aeb* is also famous for its balanced mixture of flavourful curry paste and the generous portion of fish. Although she makes four to five different versions of *aeb* every day (depending on what's available at the market), *aeb pla duk*, a version of *aeb* made with catfish, is one of her top sellers. 'Catfish,' she says, 'goes very well with the lemongrass and chilli spices.'

Rabiab's passion for cooking *aeb* is infectious. 'I can't make a lot of profit from selling them, but I'm so happy to do it everyday,' she says with a motherly smile. Unwrapping a parcel of her *aeb* is like opening a birthday gift, except with the bonus of an unforgettable fragrance of lemongrass and garlic, which pours from the wrapper. Her parcels of *aeb pla duk* are juicy from the oils of the fish and bursting with flavour. I hope my customers will '*gin im loko aroi*,' Rabiab says – 'eat until delightfully full.' ***MW***

Source //
Khun Rabiab Kamsang
Location //
home cook and
market stall, Nan

ROASTED CATFISH IN BANANA LEAF

Aeb pla duk

Serves 2–3

Preparation time: 45 mins
Cooking time: 20–25 mins

Ingredients
20 shallots
1 head of garlic
10 lemongrass stalks, trimmed,
* tough outer skin discarded*
* and sliced*
10–15 dried Thai bird's eye chillies
2 tbsp chopped turmeric
2 tsp salt
1kg catfish or tilapia steaks, cut
* into 2cm slices*

20 × 30cm banana leaves,
* for wrapping*
toothpicks, for fastening

1 In a blender or food processor, purée the shallots, garlic, lemongrass, chillies, turmeric and salt with a splash of water. Transfer to a bowl. Add the fish and mix thoroughly. Allow to marinate for about 15 minutes.

2 Prepare the banana leaves for wrapping by stacking them on top of each other, shiny side down, with one of the leaves turned 180° from the other. Add two or three slices of the marinated fish to the centre of the banana leaf. Wrap the sides first, then close the ends, making sure it's a neat and tight parcel, then fasten with a few toothpicks making sure there are no gaps. Repeat until all the fish has been wrapped into roughly 10 parcels.

3 Steam the parcels for 15–20 minutes, then wrap the parcels with a further layer of banana leaf and grill on a barbecue for about 5 minutes to char. Alternatively, you can omit steaming them and grill for 20–30 minutes on a low heat (and if so the second wrapping of banana leaves is not necessary). Eat with freshly steamed sticky rice (see page 264).

'Aeb *is an entire meal all in
one simple and delicious parcel – all
you need with it is sticky rice.*'

Rabiab Kamsang

PORK & TOMATO STEW WITH RICE NOODLES

Khanom jin nam ngiao

Khun May cooks this northern Thai pork and tomato stew, nam ngiao, *a dish that tops the list of comfort foods for many northern Thais.*

I n northern Thai cuisine, no dish is more locally beloved than *nam ngiao*, a complex stew of pork and tangy tomatoes, flavoured with a spicy curry paste and typically served with rice vermicelli noodles. *Nam ngiao* is similar to dishes in northern Myanmar and southern parts of Yunnan, China, where the dish is said to have originated before drifting into northern Thailand.

Khun May's small restaurant, a couple of tables shaded under a huge tree near the railroad tracks, is more than just a haven of delicious home-cooked food, it's a neighbourhood hangout. 'Many people come to buy my food as a takeaway on their way to work in the morning, and all my customers are repeat customers from this neighbourhood,' she says. May explains that she doesn't really need the money, but she cooks and sells because she enjoys doing it, and also because, 'I love to hang out – I don't want to be at home not doing anything.'

'I make a Lampang style of *nam ngiao*,' says May. Every province, or even town, in the north has what seems to be their own take on the dish. For instance, instead of using *tua now* – literally rotten soybeans – like they often use in Chiang Mai or Chiang Rai, in Lampang recipes tend to use salted preserved soybean sauce. And likewise, as May explains, 'people in Lampang love to eat blood jelly, that's why the *nam ngiao* you'll find here typically includes lots of it.'

When someone orders *nam ngiao*, she takes a bowl, fills it with a generous portion of fresh rice vermicelli noodles, known in Thai as *khanom jin*, then ladles on a scoop of *nam ngiao*. She proceeds to quickly top it with fresh coriander, spring onions, fried garlic and crunchy pork rinds. What really stands out about May's *nam ngiao* is the warm and welcoming aura that radiates from both her cooking and her personality. Her *nam ngiao* would make any local from Lampang feel like they're back home. ***MW***

Source //
Khun May
Location //
Market food stall,
Lampang

PORK & TOMATO STEW WITH RICE NOODLES

Khanom jin nam ngiao

Serves 8

Preparation time: 30 mins
Cooking time: 1 hr

Ingredients

500g pork bones (backbones or ribs)
125ml (4 fl oz) oil
3 tbsp fermented soybeans
500g minced pork
*3 blocks of chicken blood jelly or 500g extra
   minced pork*
500g cherry tomatoes or roma tomatoes, halved
2 tbsp light soy sauce
1kg fresh khanom jin or rice vermicelli noodles

For the curry paste

10 dried red spur chillies
10 coriander roots
10 cloves garlic, roughly chopped
10 shallots, roughly chopped
3 tsp salt
3 tsp shrimp paste

For the toppings

crispy-fried garlic (see page 264)
coriander
spring onions
pork rinds

For the side garnish

lime wedges
pickled mustard greens, shredded
bean sprouts
deep-fried Thai bird's eye chillies

1 Make the curry paste. In a small bowl, soak the dried chillies in water for 20 minutes, then drain. In a mortar and pestle (or using a hand blender) pound the curry paste ingredients, except for the shrimp paste, until you have a coarse paste. Add the shrimp paste and pound for another 5 minutes. Set aside.

2 Fill a large pan with water and add the pork bones. Bring to the boil and simmer for 30 minutes.

3 Meanwhile, in a wok or frying pan heat the oil over a low heat, once hot stir-fry the curry paste for 5 minutes until fragrant. Add the fermented soybean and the minced pork (including the extra quantity, if using), and stir-fry until cooked.

4 Add the curry paste and cooked pork mince to the pork broth and simmer for 10 minutes.

5 If using the chicken blood, add the blocks to a pan of water. Bring to the boil and then throw out the water. Repeat the process three times to clean the blood. Then slice the chicken blood and add it, along with the tomatoes, to the simmering pork broth. Continue to simmer for about 30 minutes, until the tomatoes are soft. Add the soy sauce and taste to adjust the seasoning. To serve, add a handful of rice vermicelli noodles to a bowl, ladle over the *nam ngiao*, garnish with crispy-fried garlic, coriander, spring onions and pork rinds, and serve with your choice of side garnishes.

STIR-FRIED CURRY NOODLES

Kaeng ho

Khun Suwapee Tiasiriwarodom is owner and head cook of Mae Hae, one of the most respected restaurants in Lampang. Kaeng ho – *noodles, curry and stir-fry in one – is a speciality.*

A s northern Thai legend claims, *kaeng ho*, a stir-fry of curry, vegetables, and mung bean cellophane noodles, originated in northern Thailand's Buddhist temples. In the days following a festival, there would be an abundance of extra food, and from the mix of leftovers some bright spark accidentally concocted a wonderful new dish. Whether true or apocryphal, *kaeng ho* is now one of the main dishes of northern Thailand.

Khun Suwapee Tiasiriwarodom, the owner and principle cook of Mae Hae restaurant, is well known throughout the city of Lampang for her preservation of authentic northern Thai cuisine. The restaurant, named after her mother who started it, has been going strong for over 50 years, and remains a local favourite. 'Real traditional northern Thai food is not easy to find any more,' explains Suwapee, but she ensures, 'I won't alter my recipes from the way my mother taught me.' Now, any given day at Mae Hae, Suwapee and her team prepare a variety of northern Thai dishes, *kaeng ho* being one of their quickest sell-outs.

Although practically any type of northern Thai curry can be used to prepare *kaeng ho*, the most common is *kaeng hang lay*, a dish made with pieces of tender pork in a tangy gravy of tamarind sauce, shallots, garlic and ginger. Suwapee reassures, 'I make a new pot of *kaeng hang lay* everyday, so instead of using leftovers, I set aside some fresh curry to make *kaeng ho*.'

Much of the reason Suwapee's *kaeng ho* is so delicious is because of the spice-filled *kaeng hang lay* she uses for the base of flavour. It's incredibly well balanced, slightly sweet from tamarind and palm sugar, with the shallots, pickled garlic and ginger all distinguishable in her *kaeng ho*. The mung bean cellophane noodles are soft, spongy and soak up all the delicious juices, the Chinese long beans add a crisp texture, and the kaffir lime leaves give the entire dish a citrusy zest. ***MW***

Source //
Khun Suwapee
Tiasiriwarodom
Location //
Mae Hae, Lampang

STIR-FRIED CURRY NOODLES

Kaeng ho

Serves 2

Preparation time: 15 mins
Cooking time: 5 mins

Ingredients
about 2 small bowls leftover
  kaeng hang lay (see Chang Mai
  Pork Curry, page 129)
1 tbsp oil
100g (3½oz) dried mung bean
  cellophane noodles or
  rice vermicelli
5 long beans or green beans,
  chopped
3 kaffir lime leaves, torn
fresh red Thai chillies, to garnish

1 Soak the noodles in a bowl of water for about 5–10 minutes until translucent. Drain and cut the noodles into 3cm strips.

2 In a wok or frying pan, add the oil and heat over a medium heat. Once hot, add the curry and simmer for 5–8 minutes until the sauce is thick.

3 Add the noodles and stir-fry for 2–3 minutes, until fully soft and beginning to soak up all the sauce. Add the beans and continue to stir-fry for another minute.

4 Finally, add the kaffir lime leaves, then give everything a mix one more time and immediately turn off the heat. The noodles should have soaked up all the curry sauce. Garnish with the chillies, for colour and extra spice.

'Real traditional northern Thai food is not easy to find any more. I won't alter my recipes from the way my mother taught me.'

Suwapee Tiasiriwarodom

GRILLED CHILLI DIP

Nam phrik num

Smoky, spicy and salty: it's easy to see why this dip of grilled chillies is among the most popular dishes in northern Thailand.

E ven in Thailand it's the simplest dishes that are the most delicious. And *nam phrik num*, a dip of grilled chillies, garlic and shallots pounded in a mortar and pestle, is no exception to this rule.

'*Nam phrik num* is one of the most common northern Thai dishes,' says Nitipong 'Arm' Moong Ngern of Small House Thai Cooking School, in Chiang Mai. 'It's so popular that Thais visiting Chiang Mai are expected to buy it and bring it back home.'

Although a dish revolving around grilled chillies may seem one-dimensional in flavour, like most Thai dishes, *nam phrik num* encompasses a variety of tastes. 'It should be salty, slightly sweet from the shallots and spicy,' explains Arm. 'Some people even add lime juice, or something else that will give the dish a sour flavour.'

The type of chilli used in the dish – the eponymous *phrik num* – is generally only available in northern Thailand, but according to Arm, there are ways to work around this if making the dish outside of the region: 'If you can't get *phrik num*, you can use any type of chilli that's not too spicy. If you want it to be spicier, then you can grill a few small Thai chillies and add them.'

Grilling herbs, while an unfamiliar technique to many of us in the West, is common in northern Thailand. 'You should grill over coals, and be sure not to let anything touch the flame,' suggests Arm. 'The shallots and garlic will be done first, you'll know this when they're getting soft.' Adds Arm, 'If you don't have a grill, it's also possible to dry roast the ingredients in a wok or pan.'

Nam phrik num is typically accompanied by a platter of steamed vegetables. Arm suggests going with pumpkin, cabbage, long beans and eggplant, but adds that, 'You can include just about any type of vegetable, even some types of flowers are eaten.' For a complete meal it should be eaten with sticky rice, and perhaps, says Arm, 'deep-fried pork rinds'. *AB*

Source //
Nitipong 'Arm'
Moong Ngern
Location //
Small House Thai
Cooking School,
Chiang Mai

GRILLED CHILLI DIP
Nam phrik num

**Serves 4 as part of a
greater Thai meal**

Preparation time: 25 mins
Cooking time: 15 mins

Ingredients
4–6 large fresh green Thai chillies
4 shallots, unpeeled
4 cloves garlic, unpeeled
¼ tsp salt
1 spring onion, chopped

Optional sides
Chinese cabbage, steamed
pumpkin, quartered and steamed
long beans or green beans, steamed
aubergines, sliced and steamed
cucumber, sliced
hard-boiled eggs
deep-fried pork rinds

1 Preheat the grill to medium-high. Thread the chillies, shallots and garlic onto skewers and grill until the outside is charred and the inside is soft. (You could also do this on the barbecue.) Set aside and allow to cool.

2 Once cool enough to handle, peel the burnt exterior off the chillies, shallots and garlic and discard, then place the flesh into a mortar and pestle with the salt. Pound until ingredients are bruised and thoroughly mixed but not yet a paste; *nam phrik num* should be relatively chunky and stringy in texture. Taste and adjust the seasoning, if necessary.

3 Remove to a small serving bowl, garnish with spring onion. Eat at room temperature, with sticky rice (see page 264) and steamed or par-boiled vegetables as part of a northern Thai meal.

'Nam phrik num *should
be salty, slightly sweet from
the shallots and spicy.*'

'Arm' Moong Ngern

PORK & TOMATO DIP

Nam phrik ong

A dip so good it becomes a main dish: Khun Wanda Makeweli's first pot of nam phrik ong *is always empty by midday at her large restaurant in Nan.*

Source //
Khun Wanda Makeweli
Location //
Khao Gaeng Wanda, Nan

Northern Thailand is well known for rich stews and curries, but equally as common are dips and the style of eating associated with them. *Nam phrik ong*, a dip made with tomatoes and minced pork, and flavoured with a light chilli paste, is perhaps the most popular. In the north it's a main dish, eaten with vegetables and sticky rice.

The restaurant Khao Gaeng Wanda in Nan, despite serving hundreds of customers each day, remains family owned and operated. And while the owner, Khun Wanda Makeweli, has many helpers, she is still the principal cook. 'I have many customers because I use fresh and good quality ingredients,' Wanda says with a thumbs-up.

'Some people now use the cheaper, bigger tomatoes, and also add sugar to sweeten them,' Wanda explains, 'but I prefer the smaller sida tomatoes in my *nam phrik ong*.' These are similar to cherry tomatoes and taste a little more tart than the larger roma variety, which are also available at markets throughout Nan. At Wanda's restaurant, the food is served *khao kaeng* style – where different dishes are displayed in big serving pots at the front. Although each day she makes around 20 different dishes, *nam phrik ong* remains one of her top sellers. It's so popular she has to make two pots everyday, one in the morning and one at midday.

'You can eat it with boiled vegetables or raw vegetables, but I like to serve it with raw vegetables, because I love the fresh crispness,' Wanda says. At her restaurant, a bowl of *nam phrik ong* is served with a sprinkle of coriander on top, and surrounded by thinly sliced cucumbers, strands of Chinese long beans and cabbage. The vegetables and balls of sticky rice are used together to scoop up the *nam phrik ong*, before taking a bite. The taste is tart and garlicky with a wonderful dried chilli undertone. *MW*

PORK & TOMATO DIP

Nam phrik ong

**Serves 4 as part of a
greater Thai meal**

Preparation time: 30 mins
Cooking time: 30 mins

Ingredients

5–10 dried red spur chillies
5 shallots
6 –7 cloves garlic
½ tbsp shrimp paste
1 tbsp oil
8 sida tomatoes, sliced into wedges,
*   or 16 cherry tomatoes*
2 roma tomatoes
140g (4½ oz) minced pork
salt
bunch coriander, to garnish

Optional sides

coriander sprigs
cucumbers, sliced
long beans, trimmed
cabbage leaves

1 Soak the chillies in a bowl of water for 15 minutes, or until soft, then drain.

2 In a mortar and pestle, pound the shallots and garlic along with the drained chillies, until the oils are fully released and you have a smooth paste. It should take about 20–30 minutes. Add the shrimp paste and pound for a further 5 minutes, working the shrimp paste into the mixture. Set the chilli paste aside.

3 Add the oil to a wok or frying pan and heat over a medium-high heat. Once the oil is hot, add the chilli paste and stir-fry for 1–2 minutes until fragrant. Add the minced pork, and continue to stir-fry until fully cooked.

4 Add the tomatoes to the frying pan and reduce the heat to low. Cook and stir occasionally for about 15– 20 minutes until the tomatoes are soft and begin to disintegrate. The tomatoes should release moisture, but if it looks too dry, add a splash of water. Season with extra salt as needed. Allow the nam phrik ong to cool, garnish with the coriander and serve with a selection of either raw or boiled vegetables and sticky rice (see page 264).

*'You can eat it with boiled vegetables or raw
vegetables, but I like to serve it with raw
vegetables, because I love the fresh crispness.'*

Wanda Makeweli

SWEET COCONUT STICKY RICE IN BAMBOO

Khao lam

After three hours roasting in bamboo, the coconut cream has bubbled to the top of the sticky rice, so that the first bite is sweet, soft and heavenly.

K*hao lam*, sticky rice roasted in bamboo, is one of Thailand's favourite sweet snacks. Although found throughout the country, the original version is from northern Thailand, where sticky rice is ubiquitous and bamboo grows abundantly. *Khao lam* is available throughout the year, but as Khun Nittiwadi Supromin, the owner of Lampang's most well-known *khao lam* brand, explains, 'it's traditionally a winter food, because it's heavy and rich, and it keeps us warm.'

In Lampang, the brand Mae Kamun, named after Nittiwadi's grandmother, is a label everyone recognises. In fact it was her great-grandmother who first started making and selling *khao lam* after the Second World War. Now as the fourth generation, Nittiwadi is still using her original family recipe, and cooking it the traditional way. While some *khao lam* vendors pre-prepare the sticky rice, then push it into bamboo poles to roast for just a few minutes, Nittiwadi takes no shortcuts. 'We start cooking at midnight,' she says, 'because it takes over three hours to roast.' Preserving the traditional recipe and using the best quality coconuts are what makes her *khao lam* stand out, and that's what has defended her reputation for being the best in Lampang.

Before selling, Nittiwadi and her husband slice off the outer skin of the bamboo, leaving only a thin cream-coloured bamboo wrapper surrounding the tube of sticky rice inside. This makes it easier to peel and eat, and also less heavy for takeaway customers. There are always two parts to the *khao lam*. The top, known in Thai as *nha khao lam* – literally the face – is the richest part. As the sticky rice roasts in an upright position within the bamboo, the coconut cream rises to the top, creating an incredibly sweet custardy top, which many consider the prize of the *khao lam*. The bottom, or body, is still sticky and creamy, yet not nearly as buttery or sweet as the face. Nittiwadi's *khao lam* is like rice pudding, perfectly sweet, and extraordinarily creamy and rich, with an earthy roasted essence from the bamboo. *MW*

Source //
Khun Nittiwadi Supromin
Location //
Khao Lam Mae Kamun,
Lampang

SWEET COCONUT STICKY RICE IN BAMBOO

Khao lam

Serves 3–4

Preparation time: 6 hrs
Cooking time: 3–4 hrs

Ingredients
800g glutinous rice
50g (2 oz) dried black beans
200ml coconut cream
200g sugar
large pinch salt
3–4 green bamboo poles

1 Soak the rice in water for 6 hours. In a separate bowl, soak the black beans in a bowl with plenty of water for 2 hours.

2 Meanwhile, prepare the bamboo by cutting each piece below each segment to create long slender cups that are closed at one end. Wash and air-dry the bamboo.

3 Drain the black beans, then add them to a small pan filled with fresh water and cook on a medium-low heat for 1–2 hours until soft, then drain and put into a bowl. Drain the rice and add to the bowl with the beans, stir. Set aside and rinse the pan.

4 Put the pan back over a low heat. Add the sugar and the coconut milk and gently heat, stirring continuously in one direction, until the sugar fully dissolves but before the mixture comes to the boil. Turn off the heat as soon as you see little bubbles appear at the edge of the pan, and allow to cool.

5 Take one of the bamboo poles, add the sticky rice and black bean mixture until it reaches an index finger's length from the open top. Pour in the coconut milk mixture to reach the same level as the top of the sticky rice.

6 Build a hot fire with charcoal, and set up a lean-to, so the bamboo can cook vertically, yet lean over the charcoal. Roast for about 3 hours, rotating the bamboo every 30 minutes or so, until the rice is completely cooked. The rice will expand as it cooks and the grains will become transparent and sticky.

Alternative cooking method

For those without easy access to bamboo, or who aren't able to set up their own charcoal fire, it's possible to bake the rice/coconut mix in a covered Pyrex dish in a 180°C oven for 30–40 minutes, until the grains are transparent and sticky. Make sure you leave enough room in the dish for the rice to expand.

FRAGRANT LAYERED JELLY CAKE

Khanom chan

Khun Pranee Thanachai gets up at 3 am every morning to make Thai desserts to sell at the market in Lampang. Her khanom chan, a layered jelly rectangle, is eternally popular.

Desserts are treasured throughout Thailand, and one that's available at nearly every sweet vendor around the country, though originally from the north, is *khanom chan*, a sticky layer cake. It's normally prepared with two alternating colours, one bright, like red or green, along with the natural cream or white colour of the batter.

Although throughout Thailand *khanom chan* is popular as an everyday sweet snack, it also has a significant meaning in Thai culture. The sticky layer cake is one of the nine traditional Thai sweet snacks that represent prosperity and good fortune. The layers of *khanom chan* are associated with hierarchy and progression. For instance, if someone gets a job promotion, it's a tradition to give them a gift of *khanom chan*, not so much to be eaten, but rather as a symbol of taking a step upwards.

Before Khun Pranee Thanachai started selling desserts at the local market, she was a farmer, but due to her husband's job, they moved to Lampang city, and she wanted to keep busy by doing something. She had always loved Thai desserts, both making and eating them, so about ten years ago, she decided to start selling at the market. In the small hours of every morning Pranee prepares five different Thai desserts, *khanom chan* being one of her standards. 'I like to make *khanom chan* because it's simple, doesn't require too many ingredients, and it has a good meaning in Thai culture,' she says. At the market, she slices her pan of sticky *khanom chan* into rectangles and sells each piece for just 5 Thai baht, about 10p/15 cents.

The white and bright red layers are clearly visible but melted together at the seam from the long steaming process. Her *khanom chan* is sticky and sweet, with a faint floral taste of jasmine. It has a glutinous and chewy texture, with an unctuousness from the creamy coconut milk. ***MW***

Source //
Khun Pranee Thanachai
Location //
Kao Jao Market, Lampang

FRAGRANT LAYERED JELLY CAKE
Khanom chan

Serves 10

Preparation time: 30 mins
Cooking time: 2 hrs

Ingredients

200g (7 oz) tapioca flour
25g (1 oz) rice flour
25g (1 oz) arrowroot powder
15 jasmine flowers (optional)
50ml (2 fl oz) water
400g sugar
700ml (1½ pint) coconut
  milk
few drops of red food
  colouring

1 In a large metal or glass bowl, mix the flours and arrowroot powder and set aside.

2 If using jasmine flowers: in a separate bowl, soak the jasmine in the 50ml (2 fl oz) of water for 20 minutes to release their fragrance. Discard the flowers, keeping the infused water.

3 Add 50ml (2 fl oz) of water (or the infused jasmine water) into a saucepan along with the sugar, and heat on low. Stir continuously for 10 minutes until the sugar fully dissolves and then take off the heat. Set aside to cool down to room temperature.

4 Pour the coconut milk into the saucepan with the syrup and gently mix. It should turn into a coconut milk syrup the consistency of maple syrup.

5 Starting with half the coconut milk syrup, gradually add this to the flours and arrowroot powder, stirring with your hands in one direction. Keep mixing for about 15 minutes, slowly adding more coconut milk syrup until there are no lumps of flour. The consistency should be like a thin batter. Strain the batter through a mesh or fine cloth to remove any extra lumps (if needed).

6 Divide the batter between two bowls, and in one, add a few drops of red food colouring, and mix until combined. Divide the red batter equally into four bowls. Divide the white batter equally into three bowls.

7 Place a non-stick 20cm (8 inch) square cake tin into a steamer to preheat for 5 minutes. Pour in a layer of red batter ¼cm high and steam for 6 minutes. Pour the white batter on top, to create a second layer, and steam for 7 minutes. Add another layer of red batter on top, and steam for 8 minutes. Continue adding and alternating the layers and steaming, increasing by 1 minute each time another layer is added until finished. Allow to cool completely in the tin, then slice into pieces for serving.

VIETNAM

LAOS

● Nong Khai

⑨ ⑧
⑥ ④
⑤ ⑩

UDON THANI

Sakon ●
Nakhon

Ubon
Ratana

Khon Kaen ●

Mae Nam Chi

Roi Et ●

Mae Nam Mun

⑦ ⑪
⑬ ②
③ ①

**UBON
RATCHATHANI**

Northeastern
Thailand

CAMBODIA

NORTHEASTERN THAILAND

A full-flavoured, rustic cuisine that doesn't skimp on spice

GREEN PAPAYA SALAD

Som tam thai

page 173

ISAAN SOUR SOUP WITH PORK RIBS

Tom saeb kraduuk muu

page 176

SPICY ISAAN DUCK SALAD

Laap pet

page 181

GRILLED CHICKEN

Kai yang

page 185

SLOW-COOKED BEEF IN HERBS

Tom haeng luak jim

page 188

ISAAN CHICKEN AND VEGETABLE SOUP

Kaeng om

page 193

GRILLED PORK NECK

Kaw muu yang

page 199

SUN-DRIED BEEF

Neua dat deaw

page 202

SALT-CRUSTED ROASTED FISH

Miang pla pao

page 205

FERMENTED FISH CHILLI DIP

Jaew pla ra

page 209

STEAMED CASSAVA AND COCONUT CAKE

Khanom man sampalang

page 213

GREEN PAPAYA SALAD

Som tam thai

Khun Wimon Tong-Rin has been expertly mixing and pounding plates of som tam, *Isaan's ubiquitous green papaya salad, for over 17 years.*

Chef //
Khun Wimon Tong-Rin
Location //
Som Tam Pimai, Ubon
Ratchathani

P eople in Isaan love to eat *som tam* because it's a combination of ingredients and flavours that nobody gets bored of,' explains Khun Wimon Tong-Rin, the owner of a neighbourhood restaurant in Ubon Ratchathani. It must be true, *som tam*, or green papaya salad, is the most-consumed dish throughout the Isaan region. Papayas were brought to Thailand from the Americas in the late 1700s. Now an essential part of the local diet, it's impossible to imagine Isaan food culture without them, and without the freshness and fragrance of *som tam*.

Rather than using the ripe orange variety, the salad is made with unripe green papayas, which are crisp like cucumber, not yet sweet and just slightly tangy. The papaya is peeled and the flesh julienned. Once mixed with a handful of vegetables, and a dressing of choice, it is all pounded together in a *krok*, a Thai mortar.

Khun Wimon Tong-Rin has been pounding *som tam* for over 17 years. 'When I first started, I could only sell one or two plates per day,' she says. Now, on a normal day, she blazes through 30–50 papayas, each one making about ten plates of *som tam*. She could probably make the dish with her eyes closed – her hands know the exact position of all the ingredients, which she tosses with a flick of her wrist into her giant clay mortar and effortlessly pounds and mixes.

There are many different types of *som tam*, and while locally the most popular version includes *pla ra*, fermented fish sauce, *som tam thai*, the sweeter version of the salad, is also common. Khun Wimon Tong-Rin's *som tam thai* is refreshing, the papaya is crisp, and the dressing is zesty, sweet and nutty, with just the right amount of chilli heat at the end. *MW*

GREEN PAPAYA SALAD
Som tam thai

Serves 1–2

Preparation time: 15 mins
Cooking time: 5 mins

Ingredients
2–4 dried bird's eye chillies
1 tbsp roasted peanuts
1 tbsp dried shrimp
1 tbsp palm sugar
1½ tbsp fish sauce
2–3 tbsp squeezed lime juice,
  plus extra to taste
1 green (unripe) papaya, peeled
  and stoned
1 long bean or a small handful of
  green beans, roughly chopped
5 small tomatoes or a handful of cherry
  tomatoes, cut into wedges

1 Using a mortar and pestle, coarsely pound the chillies for about 10 seconds until roughly crushed.

2 Add the sugar, fish sauce and lime juice and pound while mixing at the same time, making sure the sugar fully dissolves into the liquid ingredients. Mix in the peanuts and shrimp.

3 Use a mandoline or grater to shred the papaya. Add the papaya along with the beans to the mortar and lightly pound and mix with the dressing until just incorporated.

4 Lastly, toss in the tomatoes and gently mix everything together one more time, without pounding. Dish onto a plate, making sure you scoop out all the dressing over the salad. Add more fish sauce or lime juice to taste – it should be a little sweet, very sour and spicy.

'The som tam from Ubon Ratchathani is pungent and well rounded, with contrasting tastes of sour, salty, spicy and sweet, all unified into a harmony of flavour and texture.'

Wimon Tong-Rin

Source //
Khun Porntip
Location //
Porntip Gai Yang Wat Jaeng,
Ubon Ratchathani

ISAAN SOUR SOUP WITH PORK RIBS

Tom saeb kraduuk muu

Khun Porntip has been cooking Isaan food all her life. At her restaurant she serves an excellent tom saeb kraduuk muu, *a sour, spicy soup, fragrant with lemongrass and teeming with herbs.*

'It must be spicy, salty and sour,' says Khun Porntip as she tosses in another spoon of lime juice. *Tom saeb kraduuk muu* is an Isaan version of the more well-known *tom yum*, a flavourful soup of chicken stock and pork ribs, seasoned with lime juice, fish sauce and chillies.

Khun Porntip has been cooking since she was a young girl, learning local Isaan recipes from her mother to serve at their family restaurant. 'Everyone in my family cooks,' she explains. For over 40 years, Khun Porntip has managed and cooked at her own restaurant in Ubon – which is open 365 days a year.

In Isaan, meals are typically eaten family-style, including a range of dishes, each with a different texture, taste and composition of ingredients. *Tom saeb* is often the main soup of an Isaan meal, accompanied by other dishes like green papaya salad (page 173), some grilled meat or fish and a basket of steamed sticky rice. The soup is not served in separate bowls but instead shared at the centre of the table.

Khun Porntip's *tom saeb* is the type of broth that soothes your throat and tingles as it goes down. It has a complex flavour profile, yet is superbly well balanced. The immediate taste is of heady lemongrass, followed by the earthiness of galangal, coriander and sawtooth herb. Although the pieces of tender pork ribs (*kraduuk muu*) are delicious, *tom saeb* is all about the broth. That's where all the flavour resides. Khun Porntip prefers to serve it in a *maw fai* – literally, a fire pot – a circular elevated doughnut-shaped bowl with burning coals in the centre.

Like many Thai soups, the dish was born from necessity: making use of natural growing regional herbs, stretching the flavour of the meat with broth, and rounding things off with the most common seasonings to hand: fish sauce and lime juice. The aromatic soup steaming from Khun Porntip's *maw fai* is a perfection of the art. **MW**

Serves 4 as part of a
   greater Thai meal

Preparation time: 1 hr
Cooking time: 10 mins

Ingredients

200g sliced pork ribs (ask your butcher
   to chop them into bite-sized pieces)
1½ litres (2½ pints) water

For the soup

3 lemongrass stalks, sliced into thin strips
thumb-sized piece galangal, thinly sliced
2 kaffir lime leaves, torn
4 tbsp lime juice
2 tbsp fish sauce
1 tbsp dried chilli flakes
½ tbsp sugar
½ handful coriander, chopped
½ handful sawtooth coriander, chopped
10 mint leaves

For the chicken stock (optional) or use
   shop-bought chicken stock

1 × 2 kg (4½ lb) whole chicken
6 litres (1½ gallons) water

1 If making chicken stock: put the chicken and water into a large pan and bring to the boil. Lower the heat and simmer for 1 hour, then turn off the heat and set aside (you may wish to use the boiled chicken itself in another dish).

2 Put the pork into a medium-sized pan with the water, bring to the boil, then turn the heat to medium and cook for 20 minutes. Drain and set aside.

3 Put the ribs back into the same pan and pour in 1¼ litres (2¼ pints) chicken stock. Set over a high heat and bring to the boil, lower the heat and simmer for 4 minutes. Add the lemongrass, galangal, and lime leaves. Cook for a further minute then turn off the heat.

4 Spoon the pork ribs and a little broth among serving bowls. Add the lime juice, fish sauce, sugar and chilli flakes, then top the bowls up with more broth. Give the soup a gentle stir, just to make sure it's evenly mixed. Taste the broth to make sure it's sour, salty and spicy. You may need to add more fish sauce, lime juice, or chilli, to taste. Sprinkle over the coriander, sawtooth coriander and mint leaves. They will wilt from the hot soup, but should remain fragrant and crisp.

SPICY ISAAN MINCED DUCK SALAD

Laap pet

Khun Samai Sriprai is passionate about his restaurant's speciality: laap pet, *a tangy, spicy minced duck salad, packed with fresh herbs.*

Perhaps the most recognised contribution from Isaan to a Thai menu is *laap*, a salad of minced meat, seasoned with fish sauce, lime juice, chilli flakes and toasted rice powder. *Laap* is traditionally eaten in northern and northeastern parts of Thailand and throughout Laos, where it's a staple. There are many variations of *laap* depending on region, but the Isaan version is known for being spicy and sour, and decorated with fresh leaves of mint. For a full Isaan meal, a plate of *laap* is mandatory.

After years of hard work as a rice farmer, Khun Samai Sriprai was able to open a very small restaurant. Focusing his menu exclusively on duck dishes, Samai was able to gain a local following and eventually move into a larger location. For over 27 years now, he has been serving all things duck, including his speciality, *laap pet*. 'I wanted to do something different from what everyone else was doing in Ubon Ratchathani, so I chose to cook duck, because not many people in Isaan were serving it – it's harder to cook, and takes more time to prepare than pork or chicken,' he says. Unmissable due to the giant duck statue in the parking lot, Samai's restaurant remains famous as being one of the original Isaan duck restaurants.

Minced pork is the most common type of *laap* found in Isaan, but versions with duck, chicken or even fish are also locally popular. The dressing is thickened with *khao khua* – sticky rice that's dry-roasted in a hot pan until golden yellow and fragrant, then pounded into a coarse powder. This gives the dish a signature crunch. And it's sticky rice again when serving. Eating the combination of flavoursome meat with the glutinous grains of sticky rice is one of Isaan's most beloved combinations.

Samai's *laap pet* is juicy and succulent, with a pleasant acidity from the lime juice and pickled garlic juice, a chilli fragrance and the freshness of green onions and mint. This recipe can be made with minced meat of your choice, but for Khun Samai's authentic version, use duck. ***MW***

Source //
Khun Samai Sriprai
Location //
Baan Hao Laap Bet,
Ubon Ratchathani

SPICY ISAAN MINCED DUCK SALAD

Laap pet

Serves 4 as part of a greater Thai meal

Preparation time: 15 mins
Cooking time: 15 mins

Ingredients

300g (11 oz) minced duck
1 tbsp raw glutinous rice
2 tbsp fish sauce
1 tbsp lime juice
2 tbsp pickled garlic juice or lime juice
1–1½ tsp dried red chilli flakes
4 thinly sliced shallots
1 chopped spring onion
1 small handful mint leaves
steamed sticky rice, to serve
mixed vegetables such as cabbage, green beans, Thai basil, to serve

1 Place a pan over a medium heat and add the duck. Stir-fry for 10 minutes until meat is browned and fully cooked. Turn off the heat then set aside to cool.

2 Make the toasted rice (*khao khua*). In a small frying pan add the rice and dry-fry for about 15 minutes until golden. Transfer to a mortar and pestle or food processor and grind to a coarse powder.

3 Take the minced meat, which should be room temperature by now, add it to a mixing bowl, and season with fish sauce, lime juice, pickled garlic juice (or more lime juice), toasted rice powder, chilli flakes, shallots and about half of the chopped spring onion and mint leaves. Fully mix all the ingredients and then taste. Add more fish sauce, lime juice, or chilli as needed. It should be balanced in flavour – spicy, sour, and salty.

4 Dish onto a serving plate, and top with remaining spring onion and mint leaves. Serve the *laap* with freshly steamed sticky rice (see page 264) and raw vegetables such as cabbage, green beans and Thai basil on the side.

'The Isaan recipe for laap *is simple, doesn't require very much cooking, and it can be assembled with ingredients typically present in any local Isaan kitchen. It's part of our culture.'*

Samai Sriprai

GRILLED CHICKEN

Kai yang

Khun Somboon Wongnari, born and raised near the Laos border, travels and sells food at festivals throughout Thailand. She cooks all the classic Isaan dishes, including kai yang.

Thailand has a long and delicious history of grilling meat, and perhaps the most well-known grill recipes come from Isaan. Practically every restaurant that serves north-eastern cuisine specialises in a few items roasted over charcoal. One of the most common grilled dishes, most typically found at street food stalls, is grilled chicken, known in Thai as *kai yang*. Accompanied by a spicy plate of green papaya salad and a basket of steamed sticky rice, *kai yang* is one of the signature foods of Isaan.

Khun Somboon Wongnari is from Nakhon Phanom, a province in Thailand that borders Laos along the snaking Mekong River. Though she previously owned a restaurant in her home town, for the past ten years she's been travelling around Thailand, setting up a temporary restaurant at what's known as a *ngan phacham pi thung si muang*, a touring festival – like a circus or city fair. Along with being able to see different parts of Thailand outside of Isaan, Somboon acknowledges another major benefit. 'I am guaranteed to have many customers, as there are always many people who attend,' she says.

'Some Thai *kai yang* recipes include many different spices and ingredients in the marinade, but I like to keep my recipe simple, because I think most of the flavour comes from the slow charcoal grilling and from the dipping sauce,' says Somboon. Grilled chicken in Isaan is butterfly cut, marinated in a soy sauce mixture and fastened with thick bamboo skewers and wire, before hitting the grill. Though the chicken is cooked over direct heat, the white-hot coals are toned down by a layer of ash, to prevent flames from flaring up and burning the skin. Her chicken is grilled on both sides until golden yellow, leaving the meat tender and juicy, with a lovely smoky and garlicky flavour, and a delicious salty taste from the marinade. Although sweet and tangy sauces are commonly served in Thailand with *kai yang*, Somboon's sauce isn't sweet at all; it's rather salty, and sour from lime juice, set against the punch from the freshly pounded Thai chillies and raw garlic. **MW**

Source //
Khun Somboon Wongnari
Location //
Somboon Laab Pla Pao, food catering business

GRILLED CHICKEN
Kai yang

*Serves 4 as part of a
    greater Thai meal*

*Preparation time: 4–5 hrs (to
    marinate the chicken) plus 15
    mins*
Cooking time: 40 mins–1 hr

Ingredients

*1 × 1½ kg (3¼ lb) whole chicken,
    butterflied*
*20 skewers, soaked in water for 15
    minutes*

For the marinade

1 head garlic
2 tbsp light soy sauce
½ tsp dark soy sauce
½ tbsp coarsely ground black pepper

For the dipping sauce

3 cloves garlic
5 Thai bird's eye chillies
bunch of coriander
2 tbsp lime juice
2 tbsp hot water
½ tsp salt or to taste

1 Make the marinade. Peel the entire head of garlic and pound roughly in a mortar and pestle. (Alternatively mince the garlic with a knife.) In a large mixing bowl, mix the soy sauces, pepper and garlic, then coat the chicken with the mixture thoroughly. Allow to marinate for at least 4–5 hours or overnight.

2 For best results use an outdoor barbecue, though a griddle pan will also work. Light the barbecue. Meanwhile, thread the soaked skewer through the chicken for grilling. Insert two bamboo skewers, just inside the drumstick on both sides of the chicken, and fasten close on either side with wire to secure the meat. Do this to both sides of the chicken. This method of grilling chicken in Thailand is common so that the meat lays flat and can be flipped easily, however this step is optional.

3 At this stage on a Thai grill, once the coals are hot, they would be toned down with ash. Grill the chicken on medium-low heat for 20–30 minutes on both sides, depending on the size of the chicken and heat until cooked.

4 For the dipping sauce, pound the garlic, chillies and coriander in a mortar and pestle until coarse, and add to a mixing bowl. Add the lime juice, hot water and salt and whisk until fully dissolved. Taste and add more salt or lime juice as needed. Serve *kai yang* with sticky rice (see page 264), dipping both the chicken and rice into the sauce.

Source //
Khun Boon Thai Kraiwabi
Location //
Laap Nuad, Udon Thani

SLOW-COOKED BEEF IN HERBS

Tom haeng luak jim

At Boon's restaurant, order tom haeng luak jim, *and like an artist deep in thought, he will neatly arrange the boiled beef, and sprinkle them with herbs.*

In Thailand, beef is often considered a strong meat, and in comparison to popular meats like pork or chicken, it does have a more assertive flavour. In Isaan, beef is prepared in many ways, and nearly every part of the cow is used in a specific dish. *Tom haeng luak jim* is an Isaan dish of beef and a mix of organs, simmered with lemongrass and galangal, and served with spicy chilli sauce. It's not available at all Isaan restaurants in Thailand but only those that specialise in beef.

Over 30 years ago, Khun Boon Thai Kraiwabi, decided to open his own restaurant in his home town, Udon Thani, serving a menu exclusively of country-style, traditional Isaan beef dishes. 'I've been to many restaurants with too much variety and too many dishes on their menus – like fish, prawns, chicken, pork, beef – and if they can't sell all their food in one day, they keep it for the next day,' Boon explains. 'But I believe in freshness and quality. Everything I serve at my restaurant stems from one ingredient: beef.' Over the years, as he continued to cook and serve what he was passionate about, he began to gain a following of beef lovers.

He serves the beef alongside a common, yet unusually pungent, dipping sauce. It's salty and extra fiery from freshly ground dry chilli flakes. 'I'm not going to compromise my recipes for someone's personal taste buds,' Boon says firmly, 'I make all dishes the way I like to eat them.' At Laap Nuad, the mixed plate of beef *tom haeng luak jim* includes everything from beef shank to rumen, sliced into bite-sized pieces. The meat is tender from the long boiling process, and the flavour is well pronounced, not hidden by any strong spices, just the subtle fragrance of lemongrass and galangal. The sauce, maroon in colour and teeming with chilli seeds, is naturally sweet, and sour from the tamarind, yet the saltiness and chilli heat are the most prominent flavours. *MW*

Serves 4 as part of a
* greater Thai meal*

Preparation time: 10 mins
Cooking time: 4 hrs

Ingredients
1 × 1kg (2¼ lb) beef shank or any
* cut of choice*
1 rhizome of galangal, finely sliced
5 lemongrass stalks, bruised
coriander, to garnish
mint leaves, to garnish
spring onions, chopped, to garnish

For the sauce
2 tsp dried chilli flakes
2 tbsp fish sauce
2 tbsp toasted glutinous rice powder
* (khao khua) (see page 181)*
1 tbsp tamarind sauce (see page 13)

1 Add the galangal and lemongrass to a large pan of water and bring to a rolling boil. Reduce the heat, add the beef, put the lid on and simmer over a medium heat for about 4 hours.

2 In a bowl, add the chilli flakes, fish sauce, rice powder and tamarind sauce, then thoroughly mix together.

3 Transfer the beef to a chopping board and allow to cool, then slice into bite-sized pieces. Garnish the beef with fresh coriander, mint leaves, and chopped spring onions. *Tom haeng luak jim* is typically eaten alongside freshly steamed sticky rice (see page 264).

'I believe in freshness and quality.
Everything I serve at my restaurant
stems from one ingredient: beef.'

Boon Thai Kraiwabi

ISAAN CHICKEN & VEGETABLE SOUP

Kaeng om

Seventy-something Khun Pisit Pairaw serves local recipes he learned from his father as a child, including the legendary garden stew of a chicken soup, kaeng om.

A romatic Thai soups, teeming with lemongrass, chillies, lime juice and fish sauce, are signature tastes of Thai cuisine known around the world, but country-style, herb-filled stews are less famous, yet equally Thai. *Kaeng om,* an Isaan dish, is one such, a chicken soup, brimming with herbs and vegetables, and typically seasoned with a splash of Isaan fermented fish sauce.

Khun Pisit Pairaw, a native resident of Udon Thani, now in his seventies, opened his restaurant around 40 years ago. From a young age, he had been trained by his father to cook a vast number of local Isaan dishes. But in his youth cooking wasn't his passion; partying was. 'I opened a restaurant because I was in trouble,' he says. Pisit's party lifestyle was getting out of hand, so much so, that one of his best friends berated him, saying, 'When are you going to grow up? When are you going to take life seriously? You can make an amazing plate of *laap* and know how to cook many other Isaan dishes, why don't you open a restaurant?' Pisit says he still owes it to his best friend, who pushed him into the business: 'It saved my life.'

Thais often distinguish dishes by their flavour profile, and for *kaeng om*, it's undoubtedly a salty soup. But underneath, the mix of herbs and green vegetables give a distinct fresh taste. 'For *kaeng om*, you must include dill and lemon basil – those are the only two essential ingredients,' explains Pisit, 'apart from that, you can really use any mix of vegetables you like.' A portion of chicken stock is taken from the mother pot, which Pisit prepares at the beginning of the day, and set over a high flame, before swiftly slicing a handful of vegetables, the crucial herbs, and assembling the soup according to his father's recipe. His *kaeng om* is salty like it needs to be – almost tingling to the tongue – which the herbs immediately counter, bursting with the freshness of dill and the mellow lemony undertones of both the basil and the strips of lemongrass. ***MW***

Source //
Khun Pisit Pairaw
Location //
Doi Laap Bet, Udon Thani

ISAAN CHICKEN & VEGETABLE SOUP

Kaeng om

*Serves 4 as part of a
    greater Thai meal*

Preparation time: 2 hrs
Cooking time: 15 mins

Ingredients

50g (2 oz) raw jasmine rice
*2 lemongrass stalks, outer layers discarded,
    finely sliced*
*200g (7 oz) boneless chicken thighs, cut into
    bite-sized pieces*
*2 blocks of chicken blood jelly (optional), cut
    into cubes or 100g extra chicken thigh*
2 cloves garlic
1 shallot, chopped
7 fresh red Thai chillies (according to taste)
3 kaffir lime leaves, torn
½ tsp salt, plus extra to taste
100g (3½ oz) cabbage, chopped
*1 long bean or 6 green beans, chopped
    into bite-sized pieces*
2 leaves choi sum, chopped
4 sprigs dill
4 sprigs basil
2 spring onions
1 tbsp fermented fish sauce (pla ra, optional)

For the stock

chicken bones
*1½ litres (2½ pints) water
(alternatively use 1 litre (1¾ pints) of
    shop-bought chicken stock)*

1 For the chicken stock, put the chicken bones into a large pan with the water and boil for 2 hours. Strain the stock and set aside.

2 To make the soaked rice powder (*khao bua*), put the rice into a bowl with water and soak for 1 hour, drain well, then either pound using a mortar and pestle or use a food processor to blend into a coarse powder.

3 Now to get started on the soup, in a medium pan, add 1 litre (1¾ pints) of chicken stock and set over a medium heat to bring to a slow boil. Add the lemongrass and chicken pieces along with the blood jelly, if using. Cook for 10 minutes or until the chicken is fully cooked.

4 Lightly pound the garlic, shallot, and chillies in a mortar and pestle (alternatively, smash them with the flat side of a knife) and add them to the soup along with the kaffir lime leaves and salt. Reduce the heat to low and cook for 5 minutes.

5 Add all the vegetables and herbs to the soup along with the rice powder, whisking to combine it, then simmer for 1–2 minutes, just until the vegetables are cooked, but still crisp and fresh. Turn off the heat and, if using, add the fermented fish sauce. Season with more salt to taste.

GRILLED PORK NECK

Kaw muu yang

Khun Wilaiwan Kunipan learned to grill pork neck fillets from her father. The tender marbled pork is sliced into bite-sized pieces and served with a fiery dipping sauce.

Chef //
Khun Wilaiwan Kunipan
Location //
Som Tam Wang Kaew Saka 2,
Ubon Ratchathani

In the northeastern region of Thailand, pork is easily the most favoured of all meats, and while it's used in dozens of different dishes, one of the most straightforward is a fillet of pork neck, marinated in a soy sauce-based dressing and grilled over hot charcoal. Pork neck is a favourite cut for many Thai cooks because of its beautiful marbling ratio of fat to meat, ensuring it's always juicy and ultimately tender.

'I love to eat, and I've had a lot of experience throughout my life preparing Isaan food,' says Khun Wilaiwan Kunipan, the owner and principal cook at Som Tam Wang Kaew Saka 2, a spacious open air restaurant in Ubon Ratchathani. 'All the recipes I use are originally from my father, who always had an Isaan restaurant when I was growing up.' As an adult, Wilaiwan first began selling food from a mobile street food cart, but as sales increased, she eventually decided to open her own restaurant, kind of 'a tribute to my father,' she explains.

'Most people in Isaan, especially in Ubon Ratchathani province, don't eat foods that are too sweet like they do in central parts of Thailand, so my recipe for *kaw muu yang* is less sweet than many other Thai versions,' Wilaiwan explains. After grilling the pork neck over hot coals, it's sliced into bite-sized strips against the grain, so that it's both easier to chew and has a proportional amount of fat and meat in each bite. The pork neck is incredibly tender, with just the right amount of saltiness, and a subtle essence of ginger. Just the *kaw muu yang* is only half the dish. It wouldn't be complete without the accompanying dipping sauce. Wilaiwan's version is spicy and salty, full of dry-roasted chilli flakes, fish sauce, and a touch of lime juice for that necessary sourness. It's not the least bit sweet, but instead it's piquant and sharp to the tongue, providing a perfect complement to the tender strips of smoky pork. *MW*

GRILLED PORK NECK

Kaw muu yang

Serves 2

Preparation time: 2–4 hrs
Cooking time: 20–30 mins

Ingredients
thumb-sized piece ginger
1 tbsp oyster sauce
1 tbsp light soy sauce
1 tbsp dark soy sauce
½ tbsp sugar
300g (11 oz) pork neck fillets

For the dipping sauce
2 tbsp fish sauce
1 tbsp dried chilli flakes
juice of ½ lime
coriander leaves, to garnish

1 Grate the ginger, collecting the juices in a medium-sized bowl until you have about 1 tablespoon. Add the sauces and the sugar to the ginger juices and mix until the sugar is thoroughly dissolved.

2 Add the pork and stir so that it is evenly coated in the marinade. Put in the fridge to marinate for at least 2 hours or overnight if possible.

3 Heat a griddle pan over a medium heat. Add the pork and grill for 8 minutes on each side, or until fully cooked, but not dry. Transfer to a plate and allow the pork to rest for 5 minutes and then slice into bite-size pieces.

4 For the dipping sauce, mix the fish sauce, chilli flakes and lime juice in a small bowl. Garnish with the coriander leaves and serve alongside the pork.

'All the recipes I use are originally from my father, who always had an Isaan restaurant when I was growing up.'

Wilaiwan Kunipan

Chef //
Khun Junya Chatwong
Location //
Krua Mongkhon,
Udong Thani

SUN-DRIED BEEF

Neua dat deaw

Khun Junya Chatwong awaits the forecast of a burning hot day in order to prepare sun-dried beef, a customer favourite at her Udon Thani restaurant.

Traditionally in Thailand, before refrigeration, meat was cured and preserved to make it last longer, and this dish is a lucky remnant of that era. The *'dat deaw'* of *neua dat deaw* literally translates to 'one sun', a term referring to a single day of cloudless blazing hot sun. Typically made with either beef or pork, the meat is sliced into thin strips, marinated, seasoned, then left to dry in the ruthless rays of the beating sun from morning until evening. Throughout Thailand, Isaan is known, especially in the summertime, for its extreme heat and penetrating sunshine, supplying the perfect conditions for the process.

Khun Junya Chatwong is the owner and principle cook at Krua Mongkhon, a home-style Isaan restaurant in Udon Thani. It's a family business with both husband and son on board. Although she serves a full menu of Isaan food, one of her signature dishes, and something most tables order, is sun-dried beef. 'Whenever there's going to be hot sun, I make sure to prepare a big amount of *neua dat deaw*,' Junya explains. 'If it's a rainy day, or even if it's cloudy, *neua dat deaw* doesn't taste as good because the hot sun isn't able to dehydrate the meat.'

Once the meat is dried, there are two main ways to cook it, deep-fried in hot oil, or grilled over charcoal. Junya prefers to deep-fry, giving an extra dimension of crispiness to the dried beef. 'The meat is supposed to be quite salty,' she says, 'because it's eaten along with plain sticky rice.' Additionally, *neua dat deaw* is served with a dipping sauce known as *nam jim jaew*, a spicy sweet chilli sauce that complements the salty meat. Junya's *neua dat deaw* is crispy and dry, similar to jerky, yet thicker, more hearty, and overall a little less chewy. After a few bites the meat loosens up, releasing the pleasant saltiness of the marinade and the flavour of the beef. The dipping sauce is sour and sweet with a hint of chilli heat. ***MW***

*'Whenever there's going to be
hot sun, I make sure to prepare a
big amount of* neua dat deaw.'

Junya Chatwong

*Serves 4 as part of a
    greater Thai meal*

Preparation time: 1 full day
Cooking time: 10 mins

Ingredients
1 tbsp Thai chilli ketchup (sauce phrik *in
    Thai), or ½ tbsp of sriracha*
2 tbsp oyster sauce
½ tsp salt
1 tsp sugar
5 cloves garlic, finely chopped
*1kg (2¼) beef skirt steak or flank (or pork),
    sliced into 5mm strips*
coriander, to garnish
mix of herbs and fresh vegetables, to serve

For the sauce (nam jim jaew)
1 tbsp tamarind sauce (see page 13)
1½ tsp dried chilli flakes
½ tsp sugar
1 tbsp fish sauce
*1 tsp toasted glutinous rice powder
    (see page 181)*

1 In a bowl, mix the chilli ketchup, oyster sauce, salt, sugar and garlic. Add the sliced beef, mix well and allow to marinate for at least 2 hours or overnight in the refrigerator.

2 Take the strips of beef, and using a bamboo basket or a mesh screen, lay the pieces of meat out in a single layer and put in direct, hot sun. Leave them to dry for at least 4–5 hours (if the sun is extremely hot) or the entire day.

3 Once the meat is fully dried and looks like beef jerky, either deep-fry on medium heat for 2–3 minutes, or grill under a low heat for 5–10 minutes. The meat should be crispy and dry.

4 Make the dipping sauce. In a small bowl, mix the ingredients for the sauce together, adjusting the fish sauce and sugar according to taste. Serve *neua dat deaw* with the dipping sauce, sprinkled with coriander and any desired herbs or leafy vegetables to garnish.

SALT-CRUSTED ROASTED FISH

Miang pla pao

Assemble the speciality dish at Udon Miang Pla Pao yourself, wrapping grilled fish in a variety of raw leaves. The owner's guarantee of freshness is the fish tank on display.

In inland areas, villages are built near rivers and streams, providing both a source of water and food. Freshwater fish have played an essential role in the diet and culinary development of Thailand. In Isaan, fish is often stuffed with a variety of herbs, coated in a salt crust, and grilled over charcoal. *Pla pao*, or grilled fish, is a local favourite that is often served with a lime juice-based chilli sauce and eaten with sticky rice. *Miang pla pao* is really just a method of eating *pla pao*, involving an abundance of fresh raw greens, herbs, pungent rhizomes and rice noodles.

Khun Witsanu Potawat, the owner of Udon Miang Pla Pao restaurant in Udon Thani, is dedicated to serving extremely fresh fish. 'When fish isn't fresh, it's easy to tell, but when it is fresh, it's juicy, firm and the meat is sweet,' he explains. His restaurant features two fish tanks, where the fish, literally in the space of a minute, go from swimming to being stuffed full of lemongrass and pandan leaves and slow roasting on the grill.

Miang is a general term that means to wrap in leaves, and so it is with *miang pla pao*. Bigger leafy vegetables like napa cabbage, lettuce and wild betel leaves are used as the grilled fish's outer wrapper, while Thai basil, dill and sawtooth herb slide within along with the more pungent ingredients – raw ginger, garlic, chillies and lemongrass – which are finely sliced, to add their flavour yet not overpower. The final component is the sauce, packed with zesty lime juice, raw garlic and chillies. It is self-assembled at the table. One – or a stack – of the larger base leaves is topped with a piece of fish, a few sticky strands of rice vermicelli, and a choice of herbs and toppings. It's all wrapped together, dipped into the sauce and consumed. At Udon Miang Pla Pao, the fish is fresh and firm, and the salt crust keeps it extremely juicy and flaky. Each ingredient is flavourful on its own, but everything wrapped together creates an unforgettable harmony of freshness. *MW*

Chef //
Khun Witsanu Potawat
Location //
Udon Miang Pla Pao,
Udon Thani

SALT-CRUSTED ROASTED FISH
Miang pla pao

Serves 4 as part of a greater Thai meal

Preparation time: 1 hr
Cooking time: 30 mins

Ingredients

1 whole tilapia (about 1kg/2¼ lb), gutted and cleaned (alternatively use barramundi or other freshwater fish)
3 stalks lemongrass, bruised
1 pandan leaf (optional)
handful Thai or regular basil leaves
200g (7 oz) salt

For the dipping sauce

2 tsp palm sugar, to taste
½ tsp salt
1 tsp finely chopped garlic
3 tsp fresh Thai chilli, to taste
1 coriander root, finely chopped (optional)
2 tbsp lime juice

A combination of the following, to garnish

fresh, crisp salad leaves and herbs such as lettuce, cabbage leaves, coriander, dill, basil, sawtooth coriander, chopped
finely chopped garlic, ginger, lemongrass, shallots, chillies
generous handful roasted peanuts

1 Preheat the grill to medium-high. Tie the lemongrass stalks together with a pandan leaf (if using). Stuff the lemongrass and basil into the belly cavity of the fish.

2 Rub and pat the salt all over the fish, coating it thoroughly. Place it onto a tray and transfer to the grill. Cook for 15–20 minutes on each side (the salt crust will char). Turn infrequently, so the skin of the fish doesn't break, but remains intact.

3 Meanwhile, make the dipping sauce. In a small bowl, add the sugar, salt and 2 tablespoons hot water and stir until fully dissolved. Stir in the garlic, chilli and, if using, coriander root. Add the fresh lime juice, and give it a final quick stir.

4 Once the fish is cooked all the way through, remove from the grill, and serve on a large plate. Take a knife and slice around the top fin of the fish, then peel off the salt-crusted skin and discard to leave the moist flesh of the fish beneath.

5 To eat, pile the fish on top of a cabbage leaf (or leaf of choice), top with your desired garnishes, roll up and enjoy. *Miang pla pao* is typically served family style, as a leisure meal, where individuals assemble their own rolls.

FERMENTED FISH CHILLI DIP

Jaew pla ra

Yai Pan Duangbupah has been preparing Isaan dishes using pla ra, *fermented fish sauce, all her life. A favourite is this chilli dip, eaten with sticky rice and boiled vegetables.*

'I've been eating *pla ra* since I was a baby,' recalls Yai Pan Duangbupah, an 87-year-old grandmother, born and raised in the Udon Thani province. *Pla ra*, or fermented pickled fish, is a fundamental ingredient, both for flavour and protein, in the Isaan diet. Yai says with a huge smile, 'I eat it everyday, and unless my food includes it I don't feel *saeb*' (an Isaan term that crosses 'satisfied' with 'utterly delighted by the taste', an insight into the food culture itself).

Walk through any fresh market in Isaan, or even Bangkok, and eventually a pungent whiff of *pla ra* will catch your nostrils. Pickling or fermenting fish, just like drying meat, is an age-old practice of rationing protein, making it last over a longer period of time. Isaan being landlocked, the *pla ra* is made with freshwater fish, most commonly *pla soi* or Siamese mud carp. There are only three ingredients: fish, salt and rice bran husks. It's the ratio of ingredients and the time allowed to ferment – which can vary from months to years – that determine its quality and depth of flavour.

Although *pla ra* is consumed in numerous Isaan dishes, it is also kept rather pure in the traditional dip jaew pla ra, adding only dry-roasted chillies, shallots and garlic. 'Make sure you use *pla ra* that has been fermented for over two years,' says Yai, 'that will make the best-tasting *jaew pla ra*.'

Instead of using the sauce of *pla ra* – the murky liquid from the fermentation process which is often added to salads and soups – *jaew pla ra* uses the actual fillets of the fermented fish. All ingredients are pounded together, and finally seasoned with extra salt if the fermented fish wasn't already salty enough. 'It has to be very salty,' Yai Pan says as she takes a handful of boiled ivy gourd leaves and dips them into the communal bowl of *jaew pla ra*. The taste is pungent and sharp, not as fishy as it might sound, but slightly bitter and extremely salty, with a kick of roasted chilli that burns going down. ***MW***

Chef //
Yai Pan Duangbupah
(Yai means grandma)
Location //
Udon Thani

FERMENTED FISH CHILLI DIP

Jaew pla ra

*Serves 4 as part of a
greater Thai meal*

Preparation time: 15 mins
Cooking time: 30 mins

Ingredients

*500g (1lb 2oz) fermented fish sauce (pla ra,
or 2 cooked mackerel fillets)*
10–15 dried red Thai chillies
2 shallots
4 cloves garlic
*salt, to taste (pla ra is already salty, so it
doesn't need much)*
squeeze of lime juice (optional)

To serve

(any assortment of the vegetables below)
cabbage leaves
ivy gourd leaves
spinach leaves
choi sum, chopped roughly
aubergine, sliced
okra

1 In a skillet or wok, dry-roast the chillies on low heat for about 5 minutes until fragrant and beginning to blacken slightly. Set aside to cool.

2 Using a chopping board and a large heavy knife, take the tiny fillets from the *pla ra* and chop repeatedly to mince (or chop and mince mackerel, if using). Transfer to a bowl and set aside.

3 In a mortar and pestle, pound the dried roasted chillies, shallots and garlic into a smooth paste. It may take up to 30 minutes to break it all down completely.

4 In a bowl, mix the minced *pla ra* or mackerel with the chilli paste mixture and taste and add salt. Add a squeeze of lime if desired. (Yai Pan doesn't usually include lime juice in her recipe, but says some do in order to add a hint of sourness, which cuts through the saltiness.)

5 For the vegetables, fill a large pan with water and bring to a boil. Blanch the vegetables for 1–2 minutes or until just cooked but still slightly crisp. Serve *jaew pla ra* with the boiled vegetables and a bowlful of sticky rice (see page 264).

'For the best-tasting jaew pla ra, *use* pla ra *that has been fermented for over two years.'*

Pan Duangbupah

STEAMED CASSAVA & COCONUT CAKE

Khanom man sampalang

Khun Pornsee Sakunpong has been selling Thai desserts outside Ubon Ratchathani's post office for over 24 years. One of her specialities is khanom man sampalang, a steamed cassava cake.

Elsewhere in the world cassava might be consumed as a staple carbohydrate, but in Thailand it is used as an ingredient in sweet desserts. *Khanom man sampalang* is a simple Isaan dessert, a hearty and sweet steamed cassava cake, made rich with coconut milk, and topped with a generous handful of shredded fresh coconut.

Khun Pornsee Sakunpong, a well-known local purveyor of Thai desserts in Ubon Ratchathani, has been selling her sweet treats on the footpath outside the official town post office for over 24 years. On her food cart you'll see, written in Thai, 'Khun Yai Udom,' the name of her mother, who, as she explains, 'taught me everything I know about cooking Thai desserts and passed down her recipes to me.' With the help of her husband, and occasionally her grandchildren, she prepares traditional Thai and Isaan desserts at their home, before loading everything onto a food cart to sell in her traditional spot.

The post office, to which Pornsee has no affiliation, is located near numerous government offices. This provides her customer base: government employees, policemen, firemen and 'even the governor comes to buy desserts,' she says. 'I sell from Monday through Friday from 8am to 3pm, and I don't come on weekends or holidays – so even though I sell desserts, I have the same hours as government employees,' jokes Pornsee. Although she prepares and sells about eight to ten different Thai desserts on a daily basis, *khanom man sampalang* is one of the most popular with her customers, and it often sells out first.

Khanom man sampalang is kind of a cross between a cake and a dessert, it's thick and hearty, yet smooth and sticky. The puréed cassava makes the dessert starchy while the coconut milk contributes both flavour and a buttery richness. Pornsee's version is sweet, yet not excruciatingly so, dense and glutinous. The topping of thin grated strands of mature coconut, which have a more developed flavour and tougher texture than young coconuts, give each bite of the cassava cake an unmistakable coconut freshness. ***MW***

Chef //
Khun Pornsee Sakunpong
Location //
Khun Yai Udom,
Ubon Ratchathani

STEAMED CASSAVA & COCONUT CAKE

Khanom man sampalang

Preparation time: 15 mins
Cooking time: 1 hr
Makes: 1 x 26cm square cake

Ingredients
2.5kg (5½ lb) cassava
500ml (18 fl oz) coconut milk
750g sugar
2 heaped tsp salt
grated flesh of 1 fresh mature
 coconut

1 Wash the cassava thoroughly, then peel and discard the outer skin, and chop it into bite-sized pieces. Put the cassava and coconut milk into a blender, and whizz until smooth and creamy.

2 Transfer the cassava and coconut milk batter into a large mixing bowl, add the sugar and salt, and stir until the sugar has completely dissolved into the batter. There shouldn't be any graininess.

3 Pour the mixture into a metal or glass 26cm (10 inch) square cake pan with edges. The batter should come up to about 2cm (1 inch) in the pan.

4 Steam over a moderate heat for 30–40 minutes. Carefully and quickly remove the lid (to avoid any water from the lid falling onto the cake). Allow to rest for at least one hour, until completely cooled, at which point it will harden and become sticky. To serve, slice the cake into squares and top with shredded fresh coconut.

Eating khanom

Khanom is a term in Thai that can refer to both sweet and savoury snacks, and it's a significant part of Thailand's eating culture. Khanom are typically prepared fresh, rather than in a package, and available from food carts and local markets throughout the country. For many Thais, eating a variety of khanom, whether it be a coconut custard dessert or a crunchy deep fried snack, is a part of everyday life.

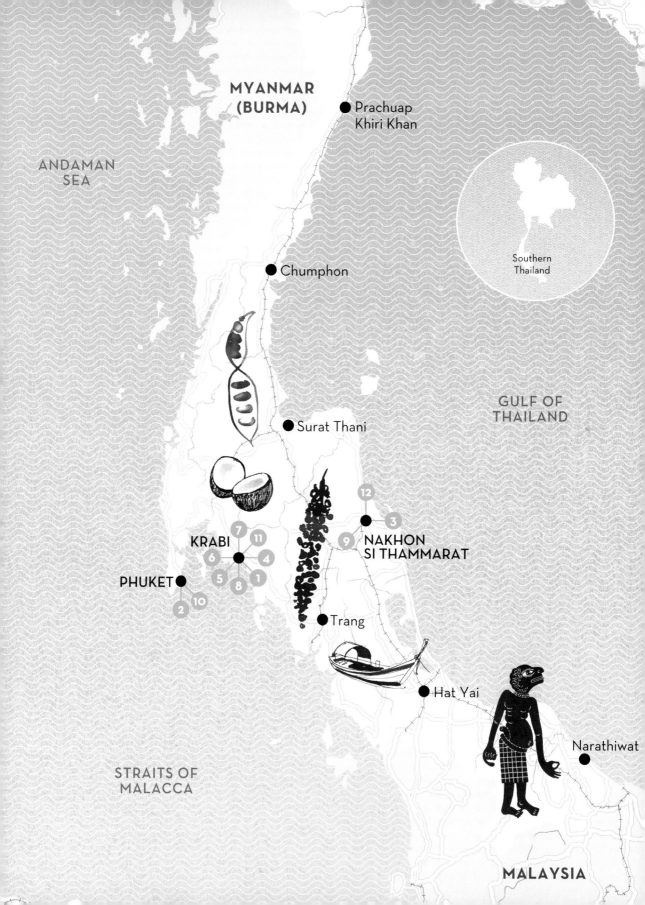

MYANMAR
(BURMA)

ANDAMAN
SEA

● Prachuap
Khiri Khan

Southern
Thailand

● Chumphon

GULF OF
THAILAND

● Surat Thani

KRABI

7
11
6
4
5
8
1

PHUKET

2
10

12

● NAKHON
3
SI THAMMARAT
9

● Trang

Hat Yai ●

● Narathiwat

STRAITS OF
MALACCA

MALAYSIA

SOUTHERN THAILAND

Thailand's spiciest offerings, with an emphasis on seafood, chillies and salt

SOUR ORANGE CURRY WITH FISH & PAPAYA

Kaeng som pla

Khun Jureeporn Damkoon is the owner of Paknam Krabi Seafood, a restaurant swimming with halal seafood dishes. Her kaeng som *is hot and sour, and glows turmeric-orange.*

If there's a single dish that encapsulates the flavours of southern Thailand, it's *kaeng som*, a sour spicy soup, usually made with fish, always packed full of chillies and fresh turmeric. *Kaeng som* variants elsewhere in Thailand are distant cousins; generally red not amber, they're sweeter and less spicy. The southern Thai version is not the least bit sweet and cooked with an exhilarating burst of sourness and spicy heat that burns, yet soothes, with each bite. For many southern Thais, a meal would not be complete without a serving of *kaeng som*.

Khun Jureeporn Damkoon is the owner of a halal restaurant in Krabi town that serves fresh seafood. As a child 'my father was a squid fisherman, and he would go fishing in the deep sea at night' she recalls. But after her father's career progressed, becoming successful in the dried squid business, 'he helped me start both a hotel and a seafood restaurant,' says Jureeporn. Hers is one of the few nicer-end, halal-certified restaurants in Krabi town, and attracts both residents and tourists.

Although Jureeporn still loves to cook, due to her busy schedule managing both a hotel and restaurant, she now has a team of three, well-qualified, southern Thai chefs that fashion the food to her specification. 'I still train the chefs and taste-test all the food so it's the way I want it to be,' says Jureeporn with a patient smile.

At Paknam Krabi Seafood, *kaeng som* can be ordered with fish or shrimp, though fish is most traditional, and with a choice of vegetables including green papaya, bamboo shoots or taro stems. Barramundi fish, also known as Asian sea bass, which is used in her version of *kaeng som*, has a soft texture and neutral taste that soaks up the flavour of the broth. The green papaya, unlike ripe papaya that's sweet, is lightly tart and crisp. The *kaeng som* broth, where most of the flavour of the soup is concentrated, is intensely sour, spicy to perfection, with a healthy dose of turmeric to wrap it up. *MW*

Source //
Khun Jureeporn
Damkoon
Location //
Paknam Krabi Seafood,
Krabi

SOUR ORANGE CURRY WITH FISH & PAPAYA

Kaeng som pla

Serves 2

Preparation time: 20 mins
Cooking time: 15 mins

Ingredients

1 litre (1¾ pint) water
150g (5 oz) green papaya, peeled, stoned
  (or bamboo shoots, taro stems or morning
  glory), cut into bite-sized pieces
300g (11 oz) barramundi or sea bass or other
  saltwater fish, cut into pieces
1 tbsp fish sauce
3 tbsp tamarind sauce (see page 13), or lemon
  juice
1 tbsp lime juice
cooked rice, to serve

For the curry paste

6 fresh Thai chillies
5 dried red chillies
5 cloves garlic
1 shallot
1 thumb-sized piece fresh turmeric
1½ tbsp shrimp paste

1 Make the curry paste. Soak the dried chillies in a bowl of water for 15 minutes, then drain. In a food processor, blend the fresh chillies, soaked dried chillies, garlic, shallot, turmeric and salt along with a splash of water until you have a coarse paste. Add the shrimp paste, and blend for a few more seconds, until well mixed.

2 In a medium-sized pan, bring the water to a rolling boil. Add the curry paste, boil for about a minute then add the green papaya. Stir the soup, wait for it to come to a boil again, then add the fish and cook (without stirring) for 5–7 minutes or until the fish is cooked.

3 Take the pan off the heat then gently stir in the fish sauce, tamarind and lime juice, being careful not to break up the fish. Serve with freshly cooked rice (see page 264).

Source //
Khun Nooror
Somany Steppe
Location //
Blue Elephant Phuket,
Phuket Town

SOUTHERN-STYLE AROMATIC HERB & RICE SALAD

Khao yam

Khun Nooror Somany Steppe is one of the top chefs in Thailand. At the Phuket branch of Blue Elephant, they serve khao yam, *a herb-filled rice salad.*

In southern Thai cuisine, there's one dish vastly different to the rest, known in Thai as *khao yam* – rice salad. While it's recognised for its health properties – making use of nearly the full range of medicinal Thai herbs – it's also delicious . Due to the array of ingredients, *khao yam* is well rounded in flavour and texture.

Khun Nooror Somany Steppe is one of the most successful and respected Thai chefs in the world. Only as a married adult did she discover an appreciation for cooking, realising not only that she knew how to cook Thai food from what her mother had ingrained in her from a young age, but also that her tongue had been trained to discern every nuance of the cuisine.

'Being a chef is always about learning,' she says, 'and this recipe for *khao yam* has a special story.' At a cooking competition Nooror was judging, the woman behind the winning *khao yam* impressed Nooror with her dish's authenticity: 'It had a perfect taste, and was so well rounded with many different ingredients.' The recipe replaced Nooror's own. 'Often *khao yam* includes a wedge of extra lime or shredded green mango to give the salad its sour flavour, but this recipe uses torch ginger flowers instead, providing a unique sour taste and texture.'

'*Khao yam* needs to be salty, sour, spicy, and with just a hint of sweetness – in that order,' says Nooror. The *budu* sauce (a fermented fish sauce, which unlike *pla ra* contains no rice bran in the fermentation process and ferments for longer), should leave no fishy scent after being slow-simmered with lemongrass, with just its body remaining. The kaffir lime adds a beautiful citrus flavour, the toasted coconut is lightly smoky and the dressing is salty and sour. But what truly stands out in this version of *khao yam* are the pink shavings of torch ginger flower, which are juicy, and add a distinctive sourness and fragrance. ***MW***

Serves 4 as part of a
  greater Thai meal

Preparation time: 60 mins
Cooking time: 30 mins

Ingredients

50g (2 oz) cooked firm white fish fillets
50g (2 oz) fresh coconut, grated
1½ tbsp lime juice
1 tbsp Thai red chillies
1 tsp dried chilli flakes
1 tsp brown sugar
6 tbsp cooked rice, such as turmeric rice, rice berry,
  butterfly pea flower rice, brown or wild rice
1 tbsp cooked rice vermicelli noodles

For the dressing
  (makes more than required for the recipe)

600ml (2¼ fl oz) budu sauce (southern Thai/
  Malaysian fermented fish sauce)
40g palm or brown sugar
3 kaffir limes or regular limes
3 lemongrass stalks, sliced in half lengthways
  and bruised
1 thumb-sized piece galangal or ginger, bruised
4 tbsp tamarind sauce (see page 13)
2 tbsp brown sugar
½ tbsp shrimp paste
¼ tbsp salt
6 shallots, crushed
6 kaffir lime leaves, torn

For the topping
  (include all or a selection of the following)

1–2 boiled prawns, or more as desired
3 tbsp torch ginger flowers (or ½ unripe green mango,
  flesh shredded)
2 tbsp very finely sliced shallots
1 tbsp finely sliced kaffir lime leaves
2 tbsp finely chopped carrot
1 tbsp finely chopped long beans (or green beans)
2 tbsp wild betel leaves (or any leafy green vegetable)
1 tbsp finely chopped green chillies
2 tbsp pomelo, segmented (or a grapefruit or orange)
7–8 leaves of Asiatic pennywort (or substitute mint
  or coriander)
7–8 curry leaves
handful of bean sprouts

1 First make the dressing. Bring the *budu* sauce to a boil in a pan on a low heat, then add the palm sugar and continue to stir for 5 minutes until the sugar has fully dissolved. Pare the zest of the limes and add to the sauce along with the juice of the limes. Add the lemongrass and galangal and keep stirring over a medium-low heat for about 5 minutes.

2 Meanwhile, add the tamarind sauce, brown sugar, shrimp paste, and salt. Add the kaffir lime leaves and shallots to the pan and continue to simmer and stir constantly for 15–20 minutes. The sauce should reduce and thicken. Turn off the heat, pour through a sieve into a bowl and discard the flavouring ingredients. Set the dressing aside.

3 In a mortar and pestle (or hand blender), grind the fish and coconut for a few minutes until smooth. In a frying pan over a medium heat, add the fish and coconut mixture and fry for 10–15 minutes until slightly golden and fragrant. Set aside.

4 In a mixing bowl, add 4 tablespoons of the dressing, lime juice, chillies, dried chilli flakes and brown sugar and stir until fully dissolved. Mix in the rice, noodles, shrimps or prawns, toasted coconut-fish mixture, the finely sliced herbs and fresh vegetables, tossing all the components together lightly.

BEEF SOUP
Soup neua

Khun Jaree Thanawut moves around the kitchen, mixing and matching ingredients; it's easy to tell she's been cooking all her life. Her soup neua *– beef soup – is a piquant delight.*

Source //
Khun Jaree Thanawut
Location //
Home cook, Nakhon Si
Thammarat

In Thailand, beef is one of the lesser represented meats, but it's the south of the country where it's most popular and commonly found. One of the favourite southern Thai ways of eating beef is simmered with herbs and spices, and peppered with fragrant chillies and shallots. Beef soup, or *soup neua* as it's called, not only stretches the flavour of the meat, but since the recipe includes such a variety of pungent ingredients like chillies and lime juice, it has an exciting flavour, and is a welcome complement to any southern Thai meal.

Khun Jaree Thanawut is a home cook from the province of Nakhon Si Thammarat, where she lives together with her family and grandchildren. 'I love to live in the countryside, because we can grow almost all of our own vegetables and herbs, some of which grow wild, for cooking and eating, and everything is organic,' Jaree says. On her family's property, there is an abundance of tropical fruit trees like bananas and coconuts, along with vegetables and necessary southern Thai ingredients like chillies and lemongrass. 'Living in the country, I can also get beef and other meat right in my neighbourhood,' says Jaree, 'and it's always fresh and local.'

'*Soup neua* should be sour and spicy and have a lot of Thai herbs and spices included,' says Jaree. Her own version is filled with the natural taste of the long-simmered stock, sweet from the bones, with a piquant sourness from the tamarind sauce and generous amounts of fresh lime juice, all with a deep herbal undertone. The fried shallots give the entire bowl of soup a sweet onion aroma, and the green chillies keep it spicy and fresh. ***MW***

BEEF SOUP
Soup neua

Serves 4 as part of a
  greater Thai meal

Preparation time: 30 mins
Cooking time: 1-4 hrs

Ingredients
1 onion, sliced into wedges
2 tomatoes, sliced into wedges
2 tbsp tamarind sauce (see page 13)
200ml oil, for deep-frying
200g shallots, thinly sliced
5 dried chillies
1 tbsp fish sauce, to taste
3–5 Thai bird's eye chillies, crushed, to taste
1–2 tbsp lime juice, to taste
handful coriander
salt

For the broth
about 3 litres (5¼ pints) water
300g beef bones
300g (11 oz) beef shank or rump, cubed
1 head garlic, peeled and separated
4 shallots, peeled
1 thumb-sized piece galangal or ginger,
  bruised
2 lemongrass stalks, sliced in half and bruised
5 kaffir lime leaves, torn
10–15 fresh bird's eye chillies, crushed in a
  mortar and pestle

1 First, make the broth. Fill a large pan with the water and put it over a medium-high heat. Add the beef bones and meat along with the remaining ingredients for the broth. Bring to the boil and then lower the heat and let it simmer for 3–4 hours, skimming off and discarding any scum that rises to the surface every now and then.

2 A few minutes before the broth has finished simmering, add the onions, tomatoes, and tamarind, stir well and allow the soup to simmer for a further 15 minutes, then turn off the heat.

3 In two small bowls, mix the shallots in one with a pinch of salt then squeeze out all the moisture by hand. In the other bowl, mix the dried chillies with a pinch of salt. Heat the oil in a frying pan over a medium heat and add the shallots. Fry for 3–5 minutes or until the shallots are golden and crispy, then drain on a plate lined with kitchen paper. Repeat with the chillies, frying until crisp and draining.

4 In individual serving bowls, add the fish sauce, bird's eye chillies, and lime juice, then spoon in the soup, mixing it with the seasonings in the bowl. Add more fish sauce or lime juice as needed per bowl. Garnish each bowl of *soup neua* with the fried dry chillies, fried shallots and a sprinkle of coriander and eat with freshly cooked rice (see page 264).

SOUTHERN THAI DRY PORK CURRY

Khua kling muu

Destined to run the restaurant named after him at birth, Khun Supphachai 'Joke' Roethong makes a unique version of khua kling, *a dry minced meat curry, overflowing with flavour.*

While most Thai curries have a saucy or soupy base, there's a curry in the south of Thailand that doesn't fit the mould. *Khua kling* is a dry meat curry: the spices, rather than being dissolved into a sauce, are directly caked onto the meat itself. It's widely available in southern regions, prepared most frequently with either minced pork or beef, and loaded with powerful flavours. Even in southern Thailand, where food is recognised throughout the country for being hot and spicy, *khua kling* remains one of the most fiery dishes of them all.

Khun Supphachai Roethong – known by his nickname Joke – is the owner of one of Krabi's most famous local restaurants, Nong Joke. It was started by his parents back in 1980, who named it after him when he was only a newborn baby. 'I grew up in a restaurant family,' says Joke, 'food has been my life.' His parents not only taught him their recipes and how to cook, but also how to manage the restaurant. Joke however sidestepped the business for a time and graduated from university with a degree in engineering. In those years, 'I didn't want to own a restaurant, because I saw that my parents were always busy, and had no free time to travel or go anywhere.' But eight years ago, when the day came for Joke's father to hand over the mantle, he couldn't resist, embracing the role he was born to.

Unlike other versions of *khua kling* found in southern Thailand, the dish at Nong Joke has a fragrant aroma of cumin, not typically used in Thai food, along with the liquorice-like flavour of sliced jeera leaves. 'Our *khua kling* is unique,' says Joke, 'and I got all my recipes from my mother, who has always made it this way.' His *khua kling* is loaded with flavour, earthy from thin slivers of galangal, balanced with the aromatic flavours of shaved lemongrass, kaffir lime leaves and cumin, and spicy-hot all the way through. ***MW***

Source //
Khun Supphachai
'Joke' Roethong
Location //
Nong Joke, Krabi

SOUTHERN THAI DRY PORK CURRY

Khua kling muu

*Serves 4 as part of a
    greater Thai meal*

Preparation time: 1 hr
Cooking time: 10 mins

Ingredients

1 tbsp oil
250g (9 oz) minced pork
*thumb-sized piece galangal or ginger,
    finely chopped*
1 tbsp fresh green peppercorns
*4 kaffir lime leaves, finely shredded,
    plus extra to garnish*
handful Thai sweet basil, finely chopped
pinch of ground coriander
pinch of ground cumin
1 fresh red chilli, finely sliced, to garnish
1 tbsp fish sauce
1 tsp brown sugar

For the curry paste (makes more than is required for the recipe)

8 dried chillies
1 kaffir lime
4–6 fresh Thai red chillies
3 shallots, sliced
3 cloves garlic, sliced
½ thumb-sized piece galangal, sliced
*1 lemongrass stalk, tough outer skin
    discarded, top trimmed, sliced*
1½cm (½ inch) piece fresh turmeric, sliced
1 tsp white peppercorns
½ tbsp shrimp paste

1 To make the curry paste, soak the Thai dried chillies in a bowl of water for 15 minutes, then drain and cut into pieces. Pare the zest from the kaffir lime and add it to a mortar and pestle (or hand blender) along with the dried and fresh chillies and the remaining ingredients for the curry paste apart from the shrimp paste. Pound or process the mixture until you have a smooth paste – if using a mortar and pestle this may take 30–60 minutes. Lastly, add the shrimp paste and pound for another 5 minutes until thoroughly combined. Set aside.

2 Heat the oil in a frying pan or wok over a low heat. Once hot, add a heaped tablespoonful of curry paste. Stir-fry continuously for about 2 minutes until fragrant and smoking. Add the pork, sugar and fish sauce and continue to stir-fry for about 10 minutes until the pork is browned and almost completely cooked.

3 Toss in the galangal, peppercorns and kaffir lime leaves and stir-fry with the pork for 1 minute, then turn off the heat and stir in the basil, coriander and cumin. Garnish *khua kling* with the red chilli slices and more finely shaved kaffir lime leaves for decoration.

DEEP-FRIED FISH WITH TURMERIC

Pla thawt khamin

Khun Jinthana Rotchanatham is the owner of Cheap Cheap Restaurant, where the smell of crispy garlic and turmeric atop deep-fried fish (pla thawt khamin) fills the room.

One of the major distinctions of southern Thai cuisine is the prevalence of fresh turmeric, a rhizome in the ginger family, that's deeper orange in colour than a carrot. One of its most iconic uses is in *pla thawt khamin*, deep-fried fish topped with a mound of orange crispy garlic and turmeric.

Khun Jinthana Rotchanatham, from Krabi in the south of Thailand, like many other Thais grew up in a household that loved to cook and eat. But despite her love for food, Jinthana spent much of her earlier life as an entrepreneur, hopping from business to business, but always with a vision for opportunity. Just two years ago she decided to pair her love for food and her business mindset to start a restaurant. 'While I was driving around the tourist area of Ao Nang, I noticed there were many restaurants, but most were expensive and didn't serve local Thai food,' she explains. 'So I decided to start a restaurant, keep the prices low, and stick with serving authentic Thai food.'

The result of her entrepreneurial endeavour was the birth of Cheap Cheap Restaurant, located just up the road from tourist central. 'I get all my ingredients locally, and I have many food source connections,' Jinthana says, 'that's how I'm able to keep the prices lower, and can still guarantee the quality of the food.' Her restaurant attracts plenty of both foreigners and Thais, hungry for authentic Thai food in an area dominated by restaurants that tone down their flavours to cater more towards visitors.

Although you can use any fish for *pla thawt khamin*, Jinthana likes to use *pla sai*, the small sand whiting fish, found in the shallow waters off the coast of Krabi. She likes it because once deep-fried 'you can eat all the bones and everything'. At her restaurant, order a plate of fried fish with turmeric, and moments later the entire dining room is filled with the aroma of fried garlic. The fish is piping hot and extra crispy, piled high with crunchy golden crumbs of incredibly fragrant garlic and turmeric, and tastes extraordinarily delicious with just plain steamed rice. *MW*

Source //
Khun Jinthana
Rotchanatham
Location //
Cheap Cheap
Restaurant, Krabi

DEEP-FRIED FISH WITH TURMERIC

Pla thawt khamin

**Serves 4 as part of a
greater Thai meal**

Preparation time: 15 mins
Cooking time: 15 mins

Ingredients

*1 × 250g (9 oz) whole sand whiting, gutted
and cleaned (or mackerel, barramundi or
snapper)*
*100g (3½ oz) purple Thai garlic or regular
garlic, separated, ends cut off and
unpeeled*
*100g (3½ oz) garlic, separated, ends cut off
and unpeeled*
*200g (7 oz) fresh turmeric,
roughly chopped*
*2 coriander roots, roughly chopped
(optional)*
½ tbsp salt
oil, for deep-frying

1 In a mortar and pestle (or food processor), grind the garlic, turmeric and coriander roots until fragrant, but still coarse and chunky. Mix in the salt.

2 Rinse the fish and thoroughly pat dry. In a mixing bowl, sprinkle the garlic-turmeric mixture over both sides of the fish, making sure it is well coated. Set aside and leave to marinate for 5 minutes.

3 In a wok or large pan, heat enough oil for deep-frying over a medium heat. Once hot, scrape the garlic-turmeric mixture off the fish, set aside, and fry the fish for about 4 minutes on each side (depending on its size, at this stage it should be 3 minutes from being fully cooked).

4 Add the reserved garlic-turmeric mixture to the hot oil along with the fish and deep-fry for 3–5 minutes until the fish is crispy and golden. Transfer to a plate lined with kitchen paper to drain. Serve the fish on a plate piled with the crispy garlic and turmeric and serve alongside hot steamed rice (see page 264).

SOUTHERN-STYLE RICE NOODLES WITH FISH CURRY

Khanom jin nam ya khati

Khun Cholaya Laothong has her students at the Krabi Cookery School pound out the paste for nam ya khati, *a fish curry served with fresh vermicelli noodles.*

N *am ya khati*, a fish curry with a rich coconut milk base and a blend of spices, is available everywhere in the south. It's typically eaten with *khanom jin*, a variety of fresh soft rice noodles, transforming into the dish *khanom jin nam ya khati*, and is usually eaten for breakfast or lunch, accompanied by *phak naw*, an assortment of fresh raw local herbs and vegetables. For many Thais, a visit to the south of Thailand wouldn't be complete without eating *khanom jin nam ya khati*.

After graduating with a diploma in food nutrition, Khun Cholaya Laothong, better known by her nickname Ya, went straight into the restaurant business. 'I can cook all kinds of Thai food from around the country,' explains Ya, 'I learned from my mother, my university education, and lots of experience and practice.' Although Ya previously served as an executive chef and manager at a number of world-class hotels and restaurants, she's now the owner and head instructor at the Krabi Cookery School, which she started in the year 2000. 'I wanted to teach foreigners how to cook real Thai food,' she says with a warm smile. In her classes, and her cooking, she doesn't take shortcuts. 'We begin by pounding the curry paste by hand, instead of using already prepared paste,' Ya explains.

'The difference between a good and bad version of *nam ya khati curry*,' says Ya, 'is the amount of curry paste and fish added.' A good version should be *tung kreung kaeng* – which roughly translates to well rounded and full of flavour. The main difference this southern curry has from other Thai counterparts, 'is the richer coconut milk and turmeric, giving the curry its beautiful yellow colour,' explains Ya. The fresh *khanom jin* noodles are silky, the perfect bed for the rich and hearty curry. Her *nam ya khati* is spicy, bursting with the flavours of lemongrass, galangal and turmeric, and an ultimate buttery creaminess from the thickened coconut milk. This recipe makes more curry paste than you need for the dish; simply freeze the remainder. *MW*

Chef //
Khun Cholaya
'Ya' Laothong
Location //
Krabi Cookery
School, Krabi

SOUTHERN-STYLE RICE NOODLES WITH FISH CURRY

Khanom jin nam ya khati

Serves 4 as part of a
greater Thai meal

Preparation time: 1 hr
Cooking time: 10 mins

Ingredients
1 × 300g (11 oz) mackerel
280ml (9½ fl oz) coconut milk
3 kaffir lime leaves, torn

For the curry paste (makes more than
required for the recipe)
10 dried red chillies
3 dried spur or red chillies
2 shallots, peeled and roughly chopped
5 cloves garlic, peeled and roughly chopped
½ lemongrass stalk, trimmed and
roughly chopped
thumb-sized piece galangal or ginger,
roughly chopped
2 tbsp chopped fresh turmeric
1 kaffir lime, peel only
2 tbsp salt
1 tbsp shrimp paste

To serve
1kg (2¼ lb) fresh rice vermicelli noodles or
cooked vermicelli rice noodles

For the garnish
(include all or a selection of the following)
2 cucumbers, sliced
Thai aubergines or regular aubergines,
blanched
basil leaves
other raw vegetables of choice, such as bean
sprouts, long beans or cabbage

1 Make the curry paste. Soak the dried chillies in a bowl of room-temperature water for about 15 minutes, then drain and chop.

2 In a mortar and pestle (or food processor) grind all ingredients for the paste, except the shrimp paste, until you have a medium-fine paste. Add the shrimp paste, then grind for another minute. The paste should thicken and become drier. Leaving 2 tablespoons behind, transfer the remainder of the curry paste into a freezer-proof container and into the freezer for another day.

3 Meanwhile, cook the mackerel in a pan of boiling water for 10–15 minutes until cooked, then remove the bones and add the flesh to the curry paste. Pound or process for about 5 minutes until well combined.

4 In a saucepan, heat the coconut milk over a medium-low heat. Add the fish curry paste and stir until fully dissolved. Cook the curry, stirring gently and continuously, moving the spoon only in one circular direction (so the coconut milk doesn't curdle), for about 10–15 minutes until it comes to a boil. Add the kaffir lime leaves and immediately turn off the heat. Serve the *nam ya khati* with rice vermicelli noodles and garnish with an assortment of fresh vegetables, either raw or blanched.

> *'The difference between a good
> and bad version of* nam ya
> khati *is the amount of curry
> paste and fish added.'*
>
> **'Ya' Laothong**

CHICKEN BRAISED IN RICE WITH TURMERIC & SPICES

Khao mok kai

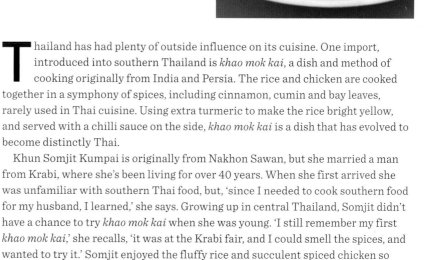

Khun Somjit Kumpai picked up her khao mok kai *recipe chatting in the market. It's chicken biryani through a Thai lens, full of spices and fragrant from crispy fried shallots.*

Thailand has had plenty of outside influence on its cuisine. One import, introduced into southern Thailand is *khao mok kai*, a dish and method of cooking originally from India and Persia. The rice and chicken are cooked together in a symphony of spices, including cinnamon, cumin and bay leaves, rarely used in Thai cuisine. Using extra turmeric to make the rice bright yellow, and served with a chilli sauce on the side, *khao mok kai* is a dish that has evolved to become distinctly Thai.

Khun Somjit Kumpai is originally from Nakhon Sawan, but she married a man from Krabi, where she's been living for over 40 years. When she first arrived she was unfamiliar with southern Thai food, but, 'since I needed to cook southern food for my husband, I learned,' she says. Growing up in central Thailand, Somjit didn't have a chance to try *khao mok kai* when she was young. 'I still remember my first *khao mok kai*,' she recalls, 'it was at the Krabi fair, and I could smell the spices, and wanted to try it.' Somjit enjoyed the fluffy rice and succulent spiced chicken so much that, 'for many years, even after we had children, we would go to buy *khao mok kai* from the same vendor every year at the fair.'

Previously she had a southern Thai rice and curry restaurant, where she catered lunch to over 100 employees at a local business. Now, she has retired, but still cooks every day for her household. Her *khao mok kai* is extremely fragrant, each grain of rice is fluffy and individually coated in a curry powder blend. The chicken takes on the same spice profile, remaining tender and juicy, while the side sauce is sweet and tangy, undoubtedly a Thai flavour twist. But what really lends an extra dimension of delicious taste are the deep fried shallots sprinkled on top, gifting crispiness to each bite. ***MW***

Source //
Khun Somjit Kumpai
Location //
Krabi

CHICKEN BRAISED IN RICE WITH TURMERIC & SPICES

Khao mok kai

*Serves 4 as part of a
greater Thai meal*

Preparation time: 1 hr
Cooking time: 1 hr

Ingredients

*3 chicken legs, skin removed, each cut into big
chunks (about 700g/1 lb 10 oz total)*
2 tsp curry powder
1 tsp ground turmeric
1 tsp ground coriander
½ tsp ground cumin
1 tsp ground cinnamon
1 tsp salt
1 tbsp sugar
2 bay leaves
*200ml (7 fl oz) canned unsweetened
evaporated milk*
20g (¾oz) butter
*500g (1 lb 2 oz) jasmine rice, rinsed
and drained*
500ml (18 fl oz) water, plus 2 tbsp
oil, for deep-frying
300g (11 oz) large shallots, very finely sliced
pinch of salt

For the dipping sauce

½ tsp salt
5–6 dried red chillies
3 tbsp sugar
2 tbsp white vinegar

1 In a large bowl, mix the spices, salt, sugar, bay leaves and evaporated milk. Add the chicken and spoon the marinade all over the chicken. Set aside to marinate for at least 15 minutes.

2 In a frying pan or wok, add the butter and heat over a medium-high heat until melted and foaming. Add the chicken, including all the marinade, and fry for 10–15 minutes until the chicken is cooked and spices smell fragrant. Transfer to a plate and set aside.

3 In a medium-sized pan, add the drained rice. Put the chicken and sauce on top, add the water and bring to the boil. Cover with the lid, turn the heat to low and cook for 20–25 minutes until the rice is fully cooked. (You could also do this in a rice cooker.)

4 Meanwhile, in a frying pan or wok, heat enough oil for deep-frying. In a bowl, toss the shallots with a pinch of salt then tightly squeeze all the liquid out of the shallots to draw out all their moisture. Add the shallots to the hot oil and fry over a medium heat for 1–2 minutes until golden and crispy. Remove to a plate lined with kitchen paper to drain.

5 Make the dipping sauce. In a mortar and pestle (or food processor), grind the salt and chillies for about 15 minutes until you have a coarse paste. In a saucepan, mix the pounded chillies, sugar, vinegar, and the 2 tablespoons of water, bring to a boil, stirring until the sugar has fully dissolved, then turn off the heat and allow to cool. To serve, plate up the rice, top with a piece of chicken and a sprinkling of crispy shallots with the sauce in a bowl alongside.

SPICY PORK RIB CURRY

Kaeng phrik seekhong muu

Khun Pong Thammavisooth's restaurant Rhythm is for meat connoisseurs. His version of kaeng phrik seekhong muu, *a southern Thai pork rib curry, is richly spiced and smoky.*

Curries are among the most beloved and widely available dishes in the south of Thailand, and *kaeng phrik seekhong muu*, a dish of pork ribs in a peppery chilli-based curry sauce, is something spicy lovers can't resist. However, while many curries in southern Thailand tend to use coconut milk as the base, which enriches and thickens the curry, *kaeng phrik seekhong muu* is instead swimming in a broth reduction.

Khun Pong Thammavisooth, who was born and raised in Krabi, hasn't always been a restaurant owner. His main business is in the meat distribution industry, where he imports high-quality frozen meats and supplies them to hotels, resorts and higher end restaurants throughout Krabi. 'When a friend decided to develop his plot of land, with a vision for a small community of condos, restaurants and entertainment facilities, he invited me to set up a restaurant,' says Pong, 'he knew I had access to good quality meat.' With the help of the owner of Nong Joke (see page 231), they opened Rhythm, a restaurant serving a mix of both Western and Thai dishes, everything on the menu made with high-quality meat.

Rhythm is situated partway up a steep mountain along the coast of Krabi, surrounded by lush karst limestone peaks. The restaurant is open air, with tables set up on a patio, overlooking the gorgeous Indian Ocean, lanky swaying palms scattered in the distance. Most people that come to the restaurant are looking for 'good quality food, a great view, and a time to relax,' as Pong puts it.

For *kaeng phrik seekhong muu*, 'it has to be spicy, salty and you must eat it with rice,' says Pong. 'We also add some turmeric, like most other southern Thai curries, enhancing both the flavour and the colour of the dish.' The *kaeng phrik seekhong muu* at Rhythm is prepared with fresh, good quality pork ribs, cut into bite sized pieces. The curry sauce is deliciously thick and spicy, heavy on the black pepper, with a dominant smoky dry chilli flavour. ***MW***

Source//
Khun Pong
Thammavisooth
Location//
Rhythm
Restaurant, Krabi

SPICY PORK
RIB CURRY

Kaeng phrik seekhong muu

*Serves 4 as part of a
   greater Thai meal*

Preparation time: 1 hr
Cooking time: 1 hr

Ingredients

*250g (9 oz) pork spare ribs, chopped into
   bite-sized pieces*
½ tsp shrimp paste
1½ tsp fish sauce
1 tsp palm or brown sugar
3 kaffir lime leaves, torn

For the curry paste
   *(makes more than required
   for the recipe)*

50 dried Thai chillies
1 head garlic, chopped
3 shallots, chopped
1 tbsp chopped fresh turmeric
*2 lemongrass stalks, trimmed and sliced
   into thin strips*
2 tbsp black peppercorns
1 tbsp salt
1 tbsp shrimp paste

1 First soak the dried chillies in a bowl of water for 15 minutes, drain, then cut into small pieces. In a mortar and pestle, first begin pounding the black peppercorns, then add the chillies, garlic, shallots, turmeric, lemongrass, peppercorns and salt and pound for 30–60 minutes to form a buttery paste. Finally, add the shrimp paste and mix and pound for another 5 minutes until completely combined.

2 In a medium-sized pan, add the ribs, cover with water, and boil for 1 hour. Drain the ribs through a colander, into a bowl, and set both the ribs and broth aside.

3 Heat 250ml (8 fl oz) of the pork broth (keep any remaining broth for another dish) in a wok or saucepan over a medium-high heat. Add a heaped tablespoon of the curry paste (freeze the remainder for another dish) and stir until fully dissolved. Add the ribs then bring to the boil. Reduce the heat to medium-low and simmer for about 20 minutes, then add the shrimp paste, fish sauce, sugar and the kaffir lime leaves. Continue to cook for 5 minutes until the curry has reduced down to a thick, dark red sauce. Turn off the heat, and serve with hot steamed rice (see page 264).

SOUTHERN THAI BARBECUED CHICKEN

Kai kaw-lae

Khun Jaruwan Sedan is an aficionado of kai kaw-lae, *southern-style barbecued chicken, bathed in garlic and turmeric, and slathered in a thick coconut milk sauce.*

Almost every region of the country has its version of grilled chicken, but in southern Thailand, *kai kaw-lae*, chicken that's slow grilled over charcoal and lathered in a rich and creamy coconut milk barbecue sauce, is a local favourite. Pattani, a province in the very south of Thailand approaching Malaysia, is where *kai kaw-lae* in Thailand is said to have originated, but it's available throughout Thailand's southern peninsula.

Khun Jaruwan Sedan has been a lover of *kai kaw-lae* since before she can remember. When she was a child the locally famous *kai kaw-lae* stall, frustratingly, was a 30-minute drive from where her family lived: 'My father would only go to buy *kai kaw-lae* on special occasions like holidays, and always on New Year,' says Jaruwan with a nostalgic smile. The flavour of grilled chicken covered in irresistible sauce, continues to be one of her favourite foods.

In southern Thailand, *kai kaw-lae* is a street food. Makeshift stalls, motorcycles with grills attached, and half barrel drum grills on the side of the road are where the dish is usually prepared and sold. Most of the time, *kai kaw-lae* is purchased for takeaway, and in regions close to the beach, people love to buy it for a picnic. '*Kai kaw-lae* can be eaten just as a snack, or as part of a full meal with a plate of steamed rice,' says Jaruwan.

Every now and then she'll prepare it for her family, who love it as much as she did as a child. 'Some people these days use flour to thicken the sauce, but for the real recipe, it should be 100 per cent coconut milk, reduced until thick and sticky – it takes more time, but it makes all the difference,' says Jaruwan. Her *kai kaw-lae* is grilled over low heat charcoal so it remains juicy, tender and embedded with garlic and orange turmeric. The barbecue sauce is packed with flavour, slightly smoky from the long simmering process, with an incredible fragrance of chilli and ginger, and a tangy sweetness from the contrast of sour tamarind, coconut milk and palm sugar. *MW*

Source //
Khun Jaruwan Sedan, home cook
Location //
Nakhon Si Thammarat

SOUTHERN THAI BARBECUED CHICKEN

Kai kaw-lae

Serves 8

Preparation time: 1 hr
Cooking time: 1 hr

Ingredients

1½kg (3 lb 3 oz) chicken pieces, such
*   as drumsticks, wings, breast fillets*
thumb-sized piece fresh turmeric
1 head garlic, peeled and separated
pinch of salt
500ml (18 fl oz) coconut milk

For the barbecue sauce

1 litre (1¾ pint) coconut milk
100g (3½ oz) dry red spur chillies
300g (11 oz) shallots, roughly
*   chopped*
5cm piece ginger, roughly chopped
2 tbsp tamarind sauce (see page 13)
100g (3½ oz) palm or brown sugar
1½ tbsp salt

thick bamboo skewers, for grilling
*   (optional)*

1 Make the marinade. Using a mortar and pestle (or a food processor), pound the turmeric, garlic and the pinch of salt to form a coarse paste, then stir in the coconut milk. Rub the marinade into the chicken and allow to rest for at least 15 minutes.

2 For the barbecue sauce, begin by soaking the dried chillies in a bowl of water for 15 minutes to soften them, then drain. In a food processor or blender, add the chillies, half the coconut milk, shallots and the ginger and blend until smooth. Set the mixture aside.

3 In a saucepan, add the remaining coconut milk and bring to the boil, stirring in one direction (i.e. clockwise) until oil begins to form on the surface – this should take about 15 minutes. When the oil forms, add the blended chilli-coconut mixture to the pan and continue to cook for about 5 minutes over a medium heat, stirring constantly.

4 Add the tamarind sauce along with the sugar and salt and boil on a low heat for a further 10–15 minutes until it starts to thicken and becomes sticky.

5 Preheat the grill to a medium-low heat. To grill the chicken, take a bamboo skewer (if using), soak it in water, then thread a few pieces of chicken onto the stick. Grill the chicken until almost cooked, then baste with a generous coating of the barbecue sauce. Continue to grill for another five minutes, then baste again, and grill for a further 1 minute, making sure the chicken is fully cooked. Serve *kai kaw-lae* as a snack on its own or alongside a plate of freshly steamed rice (see page 264).

'*I love* kai kaw-lae *because the chicken is grilled so it's still so juicy, it's fragrant from the spices, and a little sweet and a little spicy at the same time. It's such a well rounded rich flavour.*'

Jaruwan Sedan

Chef //
Khun Thanaporn Markawat
Location //
The Local by Oamthong
Thai Cuisine, Bangkok

PHUKET-STYLE BRAISED PORK

Muu hong

Khun Thanaporn Markawat's restaurant The Local brings southern Thai cuisine to Bangkok. His Phuket-style braised pork, muu hong, *is unique in its reliance on black and white pepper for flavour.*

The ethnic Chinese living in Phuket, many from a Hokkien background with roots in Fujian province, have influenced the island province's cuisine. *Muu hong*, a dish of pork braised for hours in a blend of soy sauce, palm sugar and pepper, is one such introduction.

Khun Thanaporn Markawat comes from a long family lineage of restaurateurs. 'I'm not sure how I first started loving food; it's just been a part of my life since before I can remember,' Thanaporn explains, 'and even when I was young, I did everything from go to the market, to cook, to help serve at my parents' restaurant.' After completing a culinary management degree in the US, Thanaporn returned to Thailand and opened The Local, his signature restaurant.

'Most of the recipes and dishes I cook, I learned from my parents,' recalls Thanaporn, 'and my grandparents taught me a lot about how different ingredients pair well together, both for the authentic Thai flavour and culturally – for instance watermelon can be eaten with rice, because it's a balance of hot and cold.'

Muu hong should be 'salty and sweet, and it's important to use good quality pepper and coriander roots, so the flavour really absorbs into the meat'. *Muu hong* does not include strong spices; instead it relies on black and white pepper to give the dish its flavour, along with soy sauce, palm sugar, and the slow braising method which increases the pork's richness. Although *muu hong* is sometimes prepared with chicken eggs, or even no eggs at all, Thanaporn prefers duck eggs – 'for a better colour, and richer flavour'. Thanaporn's *muu hong* includes a trio of different cuts of pork – each fall-apart tender – graciously coated in the dark sauce of the slow braise. The peppery sauce, reduced into a thick gravy, has a sweetness that is immediately countered by the salty soy sauce. **MW**

Serves 4 as part of a
  greater Thai meal

Preparation time: 30 mins
Cooking time: 3-4 hrs

Ingredients

300g (11 oz) mixed pork belly, loin and
  tenderloin, cut into bite-sized cubes
1 tbsp oil
1½ tbsp oyster sauce
2 tbsp Maggi seasoning sauce
1½ tbsp dark soy sauce
2 tbsp light soy sauce
2 tbsp palm or brown sugar
500ml–1 litre (18 fl oz– 1¾ pint) chicken
  stock or water
2 duck or hen eggs, hard-boiled
4 quail eggs, hard-boiled (optional)

For the peppercorn paste

5 shallots, roughly chopped
2 large cloves garlic
3 coriander roots
1 tbsp black peppercorns
1 tbsp white peppercorns

1 In a mortar and pestle, grind the shallots, garlic, coriander roots and both white and black peppercorns. Pound for about 15 minutes, until you have a coarse paste.

2 Put a pan over a low heat, add the oil and once hot, add the paste and temper in the oil for a few minutes until fragrant, which will enhance the flavour.

3 Add the pork and fry for 5 minutes, then season with oyster sauce, Maggi seasoning, dark and light soy sauces. Add the sugar and stir until fully dissolved. Add 300ml (½ pint) of the chicken stock and simmer for about 1 hour, adding more stock as needed so that the sauce doesn't dry out.

4 Add the eggs to the pan with the pork and simmer for a further 1½ hours until the pork is falling apart and meltingly tender. Keep adding a little chicken stock or water to the pan as the sauce reduces. Serve with hot steamed rice (see page 264).

'It's important to use good quality
pepper and coriander roots, so the flavour
really absorbs into the meat.'

Thanaporn Markawat

COCONUT & TARO PUDDING

Khanom takoh

Khun Narissara Pumchat used to help her mother wrap sweet snacks in banana and pandan leaves at the family restaurant, where the salty coconut dessert khanom takoh *was a favourite.*

While coconuts are available throughout much of Thailand, the southern peninsula, where the climate is tropical year-round, produces the best quality with the highest fat content. *Khanom takoh* is a Thai dessert that takes advantage of the bounty of fresh coconuts. But rather than just a single smooth pudding texture, *khanom takoh* has a base of sweetened taro or sometimes sweet corn, made sticky with mung bean flour. The base is usually super sweet, while the coconut pudding on top is instead salty, the two contrasting and complementing each other exceptionally well, while the salty pudding enhances the flavour of the coconut. Although many other Thai desserts contain coconut milk, *khanom takoh* is for serious coconut lovers with perhaps the most powerful coconut flavour of any.

Born to a mother who had a restaurant serving southern Thai *khao kaeng*, or rice and curry, Khun Narissara Pumchat was surrounded by food and a restaurant lifestyle from an early age. 'At most curry restaurants in southern Thailand, they also have some small desserts and snacks available at the front of the restaurant,' says Narissara. 'Our family restaurant was no different. One of my favourite things to do growing up was help my mother make the sweet snacks. I always enjoyed wrapping desserts in banana leaves and tasting everything.' Now, Narissara mostly makes desserts on special occasions or when she's really craving something in particular, but she's still armed with her mother's recipes, 'and I especially love to make and eat *khanom takoh*,' she says excitedly.

Khanom takoh can be eaten like pudding, using a spoon to scoop out bites, but some like to squeeze the little cups from the bottom and slurp up a mouthful. '*Khanom takoh* is fragrant from pandan leaves, sweet, and extremely rich from coconut milk,' says Narissara, 'and that's why I love it so much.' ***MW***

Source //
Khun Narissara Pumchat
Location //
Krabi

COCONUT & TARO PUDDING
Khanom takoh

Makes about 40 cups

Preparation time: 30 mins
Cooking time: 30 mins

Ingredients
2 pandan leaves
350ml (12 fl oz) water
100g taro
35g (1¼ oz) mung bean flour
100g (3½ oz) sugar
400ml (14 oz) coconut milk
25g rice flour
1 tsp salt

banana leaves, or paper cupcake cases,
   for wrapping

1   In a medium-sized pan, add the pandan leaves and water. Place over a medium-low heat for about 15 minutes – just so the pandan leaves release their fragrance. Remove the leaves and set the infused water aside.

2   Peel off the outer skin of the taro, dice into small ½cm squares and steam in a separate pan over boiling water for about 20 minutes or until soft.

3   In a saucepan, add the reserved pandan water, mung bean flour and sugar and cook over a low heat, stirring constantly for about 5 minutes until all the ingredients are fully dissolved. Then add the steamed taro, simmer for another 2 minutes, put the lid on and keep it on a very low heat.

4   In a separate saucepan, mix the coconut milk, rice flour and salt over a medium heat. Bring to the boil and simmer, stirring continuously for 5 minutes until the mixture thickens.

5   Take the banana leaves and fasten them into small cups with toothpicks (or staples as is common in Thailand), about the size of a shallow espresso cup. Alternatively, use paper cupcake cases. Working quickly, take the taro mixture off the heat and add a spoonful of this onto the banana leaf, spreading it evenly along the bottom. Top with a spoonful of the coconut milk reduction, which should cover the taro mixture like a thick layer of frosting. Both layers should still be hot when assembling to ensure that they stick together.

6   Allow to cool for about half an hour, and both layers should settle, thicken, and stick together.

COCONUT & RICE DESSERT DUMPLINGS

Khanom kho

If invited to a wedding near Nakhon Si Thammarat, you can hope Khun Jaree Thanawut has catered, providing her famous khanom kho, *sweet dumplings rolled in fresh coconut.*

One of the most widely available desserts in southern Thailand is *khanom kho*, sticky rice flour dumplings, stuffed in the centre with a cube of palmyra palm sugar, and rolled in fresh shreds of coconut flesh. The sweet dessert is found at markets and food stalls, and since it's relatively easy to cook with common household ingredients, it's popular to make at home. The round dumplings, about the size of large gumballs, are often prepared in different colours – purple, blue, red, green – or just the natural off-white colour, and are certainly a favourite for many in the south of Thailand.

Khun Jaree Thanawut is from Nakhon Si Thammarat, a province on the Gulf side of the southern Thai peninsula. She lives, along with her family and grandchildren, in the countryside, surrounded by lush forest, rubber trees and an abundance of tropical fruit trees. Although her family's main business is their rubber tree plantation, Jaree has a reputation for being one of the best home-style cooks in the area. 'Some friends and relatives will occasionally hire me to cook for large celebrations or festivals, like weddings or holiday parties,' she says. 'When I make food for a big party, I always make *khanom kho* for dessert. It's easy and fun to make, and everyone loves it.'

'It's best to eat *khanom kho* when it's fresh,' Jaree explains, 'not only because it tastes best, but also because the fresh coconut will turn sour if you wait too long to eat it.' The outer coating of grated coconut is rich and oily, and so fresh it has a natural crispness to it. The wrapping, made of just water and sticky rice flour, is soft and slightly sticky. The sweetness of *khanom kho* comes only from the inside, where a piece of palmyra palm sugar is planted, and provides a nutty caramel flavour and a little crunch. A hint of saltiness added to the outer shreds of coconut, enhances the flavour of the sweet core. ***MW***

Chef //
Khun Jaree Thanawut
Location //
Nakhon Si Thammarat

COCONUT & RICE DESSERT DUMPLINGS

Khanom kho

**Makes 100 balls – 50 white,
50 purple**

Preparation time: 15 mins
Cooking time: 1 hr

Ingredients
*handful butterfly pea flowers
    or few drops purple food
    colouring*
200g (7 oz) glutinous rice flour
*200g palmyra palm sugar or
    coconut palm sugar*
*1 fresh mature coconut, flesh
    only, grated (or use 140g (5 oz)
    dessicated coconut)*
½ tbsp salt
2 pandan leaves, tied into a knot

1 If using the butterfly pea flowers, soak them in a bowl in 60ml water for 20 minutes. If using food colouring, add a few drops to a bowl with 60ml water.

2 Put 100g of the flour into the bowl with the coloured water and the other half into a bowl along with 60ml water. Working as two separate mixtures, stir and knead for about 5 minutes. The dough should be quite sticky.

3 If using, cut the palmyra palm sugar into small ½cm (¼inch) cubes and set aside. Spread the grated fresh coconut out onto a baking tray and mix in the salt. Set aside.

4 Divide the dough into 100 even-sized balls, each roughly the size of a chocolate truffle, and then form each ball into a disc. Place a cube of sugar in the centre. Ease the dough up and around the sugar and pinch firmly at the top to create an even seal. Repeat with the remaining dough.

5 Half-fill a medium-sized pan with water and add the pandan leaves (if using). Bring the water to a rolling boil and add the dessert balls in batches of about 7–8. Cook over a rolling boil for 3–5 minutes or until the balls float to the surface of the water. Use a slotted spoon to fish the balls out of the water, drain them well and transfer immediately to the baking tray with the shredded coconut. Roll the balls in the coconut until fully coated. Allow the *khanom kho* to rest for about 5 minutes before eating.

*'It's a great Thai dessert to teach
kids, because they always enjoy
adding the little cubes of sugar to the
rice flour dough, and rolling them
into small dumplings.'*

Jaree Thanawut

BASIC RECIPES

STICKY RICE

Sticky rice is a ubiquitous addition to curries, soups and salads in the northern regions of Thailand.

Serves 4

Ingredients
500g (18 oz) glutinous rice
water

1 Soak the sticky rice for 4–5 hours, or overnight.

2 Place the rice into a bamboo steamer, or any type of steamer. Cover the steamer with a lid.

3 Steam for 15 minutes on a medium heat until soft and fluffy.

4 Enjoy while it's hot and fresh.

STEAMED RICE

In central and southern Thailand, jasmine rice is the staple, but any freshed steamed rice will complement dishes from these regions well.

Serves 4

Ingredients
300g (11 oz) rice
water

1 Rinse the rice until the water runs clear.

2 If you have a rice cooker, use 1.5 parts water to 1 part rice. Combine the two and set the cooker at its normal setting.

3 If cooking in a pan, use 2 parts water to 1 part rice. Place on a high heat until the water boils, then turn down to low and cook, covered, for 15 minutes.

4 When cooked, remove from heat and fluff with a fork to separate the grains.

CRISPY-FRIED GARLIC

Often added as a garnishing to Thai salads, soups and curries.

Serves 4

Ingredients
4 tbsp oil
4 cloves garlic, crushed

1 Add the oil to a wok or large pan and place over a medium heat. When hot, add the crushed garlic and fry briefly until golden and crispy. Remove the garlic, leaving the oil behind, and drain on kitchen paper.

CRISPY-FRIED SHALLOTS

Often added as a garnishing to Thai salads, soups and curries.

Serves 4

Ingredients
8 tbsp oil
4 shallots, thinly sliced

1 Heat the oil in a frying pan over a medium heat and add the shallots. Fry for 3–5 minutes or until the shallots are golden and crispy, then drain on a plate lined with kitchen paper.

RECIPE SOURCES

Achareeya 'Nai Noi' Boonyaboosaya, pastry chef (pp110–113)

Amara 'Aum' Chaiprasert, Le Grand Lanna, Chiang Mai (pp120–125) www.dharadhevi.com +66 53 888 888

Amornsri Pattanasitdanggul, home cook, Bangkok (pp44–47)

Boon Thai Kraiwabi, Laap Nuad, Mak Khaeng, Udon Thani (pp188–189) +66 (0) 42 328 172

Chalatwan 'Pan' Wasasamit, street stall cook, Bangkok (pp70–73)

Cholaya 'Ya' Laothong, Krabi Cookery School, Ao Nang, Krabi (pp238–241) www.krabicookeryschool.com + 66 (0) 75 662 155

Duangporn 'Bo' Songivsava, Bo.lan, Bangkok (pp92–95, 114–115) www.bolan.co.th +66 (2) 2602 962

Eakachai Matthakij, Soul Food Mahanakorn, Bangkok (pp20–23) www.soulfoodmahanakorn.com +66-(0)-2714-7708

Ian Kittichai, Issaya Siamese Club, Bangkok (pp48–51, 100–103) www.issaya.com +66 (0)2 672 9040-1

Jaree Thanawut, home cook, Nakhon Si Thammarat (p224–227, 260–263)

Jaruwan Sedan, home cook, Nakhon Si Thammarat (pp250–252)

Jinthana Rotchanatham, Cheap Cheap Restaurant, Ao Nang, Krabi (pp234–236)

Junob Tongdee, Kao Jao Market, Lampang (pp136–139)

Junya Chatwong, Krua Mongkhon, Udong Thani (pp202–203)

Jureeporn Damkoon, Paknam Krabi Seafood, Krabi (pp218–221) www.paknamkrabiseafood.com

Mallika Thamwattana, Ruen Mallika, Bangkok (pp56–59) www.ruenmallika.com +66 02-663-3211-2

Khun May, Soi Rotfai, market stall in Lampang (pp144–147)

Morten Nielsen, Benjarong, Bangkok (pp82–85) www.dusit.com/dusitthani/bangkok +66 (0) 2200 9000

Narissara Pumchat, home cook, Krabi (pp256–259)

Nathamon Jaidet, Poj Spa Kar, Bangkok (pp74–77) +66 2 222 2686

Nitipong 'Arm' Moong Ngern, Small House Cooking School, Chiang Mai (pp132–135, 154–157) www.chiangmaithaicooking.com +66 09-567-4455-0

Nittiwadi Supromin, Khao Lam Mae Kamun, Lampang (pp162–165)

Nooror Somany Steppe, Blue Elephant, Bangkok (pp52–53) and Phuket (pp222–223) www.blueelephant.com

Pan Duangbupah, Udon Thani (pp208–211)

Phatsakorn 'Toto' Tatiyaphak, Celadon, Bangkok (pp32-33) www.sukhothai.com/Dining/Celadon +66 (0) 2344 8888

Pisit Pairaw, Doi Laap Bet, Udon Thani (pp192–195)

Piyawadi Jantrupon, Amita Thai Cooking Class, Thonburi (pp104–107) www.amitathaicooking.com + 66 (2) 466 8966

Pong Thammavisooth, Rhythm Restaurant, 7-Heaven, Krabi (pp246–249)

Pongsak Siriphan, Ruen Tamarind, Chiang Mai (pp128–131) +66 53 418 896

Pornsee Sakunpong, Khun Yai Udom, dessert food cart, Ubon Ratchathani (pp212–215)

Khun Porntip, Porntip Gai Yang Wat Jaeng, Ubon Ratchathani (pp176–177)

Porntippa Rayananonda, Klang Soi Restaurant, Bangkok (pp28–31)

Pranee Thanachai, Kao Jao Market, Lampang (pp166–169)

Rabiab Kamsang, Aeb Pa Nun, market stall in Nan (pp140–143)

Saiyuud 'Poo' Diwong, Cooking with Poo by Helping Hands, Bangkok (pp36–39, 78–79)
www.cookingwithpoo.com
+66 (0)80 434 8686

Samai Sriprai, Baan Hao Laap Bet, Ubon Ratchathani (pp180–183)

Samruay Choothong, street stall cook, Bangkok (pp66–69)

Sanusi Mareh, Silom Thai Cooking School, Bangkok (p12–13, 16–19)
www.bangkokthaicooking.com +66 (0)84 726 5669

Somboon Wongnari, Somboon Laab Pla Pao, food catering business (pp184–186)

Somjit Kumpai, home cook, Krabi (pp242–245)

Supphachai 'Joke' Roethong, Nong Joke, Krabi (pp230–233)
+66 (0)75 611 639

Suthep Chutsiriyingyong, Piang Kee, Bangkok (pp62–65)

Suwapee Tiasiriwarodom, Mae Hae, Lampang (pp148-151)
+66 (0)54 221904
Tanongsak 'Dtong' Yordwai, nahm, Bangkok (pp96–99)
www.comohotels.com/metropolitanbangkok/dining/nahm

Thanaporn Markawat, The Local by Oamthong Thai Cuisine, Bangkok (pp254–255)
www.thelocalthaicuisine.com
+66 (0) 2 664 0664

Vichit Mukura, Khao, Bangkok (pp40–43)

Walit Sitthipan, Sampran Riverside, Nakhon Pathom (pp86–89)
www.sampranriverside.com

Wanda Makeweli, Khao Gaeng Wanda, Nan (pp158-161)

Wilaiwan Kunipan, Som Tam Wang Kaew Saka 2, Ubon Ratcha-Thani (pp198–201)

Wimon Tong-Rin, Som Tam Pimai, Ubon Ratchathani (pp172–175)
+66 (0)897208101

Witsanu Potawat, Udon Miang Pla Pao, Udon Thani (pp204–207)
+66 (0)93 996 1465

Yupin MacLeod, home cook, Bangkok (pp24–25)

ABOUT THE AUTHORS

Austin Bush came to Thailand in 1999 as part of a language study programme hosted by Chiang Mai University. The lure of city life, employment and spicy food eventually led Austin to Bangkok. City life, employment and spicy food have managed to keep him there since. Austin is a writer and photographer who often covers food, and has contributed to more than 25 titles for Lonely Planet, as well as several other media outlets.

Mark Wiens bought a one-way ticket to Thailand after graduating from college in the US, with nothing on his schedule other than a hunger to eat as much as he could. He can still remember his first evening walk through Bangkok – a culinary wonderland unfolding before his eyes. A short trip to Southeast Asia turned into years of eating, travelling and discovery. To his wife, Jaruwan Wiens, whom he met on his travels, he extends his thanks for all her help and support.

Samples of Austin's work can be seen at *www.austinbushphotography.com*.

Mark blogs about Thai food at *www.eatingthaifood.com* and shares food adventures on *www.migrationology.com*.

GLOSSARY

Asian pennywort
Leaf used in soft drinks, stewed into tea or eaten raw in salads.

bird's eye chillies
One of the hottest chillies used in Thai cooking. The small, tapering fruits are very spicy but have a fruity flavour and are commonly used in curries and salads.

budu sauce
Fermented fish sauce used in southern Thailand, derived from anchovies mixed with salt. Used as a flavouring, or eaten with fish, rice or raw vegetables.

coconut milk/cream
Liquid derived from the grated meat of a brown coconut. Not to be confused with coconut water, the clear liquid inside a green coconut.

coconut, mature
Otherwise known as a brown coconut. Produces thick, flavourful meat, but little water.

coconut, young
Otherwise known as a white or green coconut. Produces more water than the mature (brown) variant. The meat of the young coconut is soft and gel-like.

coriander (cilantro)
Leafy herb used commonly in Asian cooking.

fermented fish sauce (pla ra)
Popular sauce in northeastern Thai (Isaan) cooking, made by pickling several varieties of fish.

galangal
Similar in appearance and flavour to root ginger, this ingredient is used in many Thai dishes, especially curries.

holy basil
With a spicy, peppery flavour that resembles cloves, this is the most popular basil-like herb used in Thai cooking. Features in many chicken, pork and seafood dishes.

kaffir lime
Green fruit noted for its sharp, aromatic flavour. The juice is too strong for use in food, but the rind is used in curry paste. The leaves can also be used.

krachai (fingerroot, lesser ginger, Chinese key)
Finger-like root with a distinct flavour, milder than ginger or galangal. Most often used in fish dishes or curry pastes, or for adding flavour to rice.

lotus root
Diverse vegetable with a creamy, starchy texture similar to taro root, which retains its crisp, tender texture however it is cooked.

ma euk (hairy aubergine)
Known in English as hairy aubergine/ eggplant, this fruit has a sour flavour.

morning glory (phak bung)
Also known as Siamese watercress or

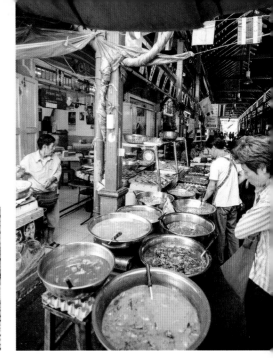

water spinach. The long dark stems are often eaten raw in salads, or cooked in stir fries or curries.

palmyra palm sugar
Made from the sap of the palmyra palm, which is boiled down to syrup that is allowed to crystallised. Mainly used in sweets and desserts, but can also be used in curries and sauces.

pandan leaves (pandanus leaves)
Plant with long green leaves resembling but not related to the palm. Used as a natural flavouring, sweetener and green colouring. Can be turned into a paste.

pea aubergine (pea eggplant)
Marble-sized variant of the aubergine (eggplant), extremely bitter in flavour. Typically cooked whole in Thai curries and soups.

pickled garlic juice
Common ingredient in many Thai dishes, especially those originating in central and northern Thailand.

roasted chilli paste (*nam phrik phao*)
Medium hot red chilli paste sweetened with sugar and tamarind. Popular on bread or toast.

salak (snake fruit)
Also known as snake fruit because of the scaly appearance of its skin, this fruit is juicy, sweet and sour.

sawtooth coriander
Herb with serrated-edged leaves, originally from Central and South America but popular in Thai cooking for its strong coriander flavour. Often left uncooked.

shrimp paste
Common ingredient in all southeast Asian cooking made from fermented ground shrimp. Two variations used in southern Thai cooking include one where the shrimp is mixed with fish, and another that is sweet.

spur chillies
Long, brightly coloured chillies of medium heat by the standards of

Thai cooking. Commonly roasted in northern Thailand.

tamarind pulp/sauce
Sweet and sour ingredient, a key constituent in pad thai sauce. The riper the tamarind, the sweeter and less sour the pulp (to the extent where it is even used in desserts). See also page 13.

Thai aubergine (Thai eggplant)
Southeast Asian variant of the aubergine (eggplant) dish, green-white in colour and egg-sized. Often eaten raw in salads or as garnishes.

Thai basil
With a slightly spicy flavour resembling licorice, this is a frequent ingredient in curries.

turmeric
Plant native to India and the spice derived from it. Typically used in its dried, powdered form but can be used fresh, like ginger (particularly in southern Thai cooking).

INDEX

Published in August 2015 by Lonely Planet Publications Pty Ltd
ABN 36 005 607 983
www.lonelyplanet.com
ISBN 978 1 7436 0763 3
© Lonely Planet 2015
Printed in China
Written by Austin Bush and Mark Wiens

Publishing Director Piers Pickard
Commissioning Editor Jessica Cole
Copyeditors Kate Wanwimolruk and Nick Ascroft
Art Direction Daniel Di Paolo
Layout Designer Amanda Scope
Illustrator Louise Sheeran
Cartographer Wayne Murphy
Pre-press Production Tag Publishing
Print Production Larissa Frost, Nigel Longuet

With thanks to the recipe testers: Aaron London, Adel Smee, Alexandria DeVera, Amanda McAdams, Amy Lysen, Anna Harris, Brendan Dempsey, Britney Alvarez, Cate Jacques, Claire Beyer, Clara Monitto, Clive Shepherd, Ding Ziling, Ellie Simpson, Emily Farthing, Florian Poppe, Gemma Graham, Georgina Leslie, Ivey Hanson, Jane Atkin, Jen Feroze, Jessica Rose, Joe Bindloss, Josh Mahoney, Justin Morris, Kate Dumbrell, Laura Noiret, Lauren Wellicome, Lorna Parkes, Luisa Cosio, Luna Soo, Madeleine diBiasi, Martine Power, Matt Parish, Matt Phillips, Natalie Nicolson, Nicole Griffith, Rana Freedman, Rick Wiebusch, Ronald Tjoeka, Ruth Cosgrove, Samantha Russell-Tulip, Sarah Anthony, Sasha Baskett, Scott Stampfli, Seb Neylan, Shahara Ahmed.

Picture credits

All images and text on pages 2, 3, 4, 7, 8, 12–117, 121–134, 154-7 and 264, and images on pages 268–9, by Austin Bush. All images and text on pages 136–151, 154–169, 172–177, 180–189, 192–195, 198–215, 218–227, 230–236 and 238–252 by Mark Wiens. Getty images: 152–153, 178–179, 190–191, 196–197, 228–229, 253. Lonely Planet Images: 237. Front cover: Austin Bush (top right, bottom left); Mark Wiens (bottom right). Back cover: Austin Bush (top, centre), Lonely Planet Images (bottom).

Lonely Planet offices

AUSTRALIA
90 Maribyrnong St, Footscray, Victoria, 3011, Australia
Phone 03 8379 8000 Email talk2us@lonelyplanet.com.au

USA
150 Linden St, Oakland, CA 94607
Phone 510 250 6400 Email info@lonelyplanet.com

UNITED KINGDOM
240 Blackfriars Road, London SE1 8NW
Phone 020 3771 5100 Email go@lonelyplanet.co.uk

Although the authors and Lonely Planet have taken all reasonable care in preparing this book, we make no warranty about the accuracy or completeness of its content and, to the maximum extent permitted, disclaim all liability from its use.

Paper in this book is certified against the Forest Stewardship Council™ standards. FSC™ promotes environmentally responsible, socially beneficial and economically viable management of the world's forests.

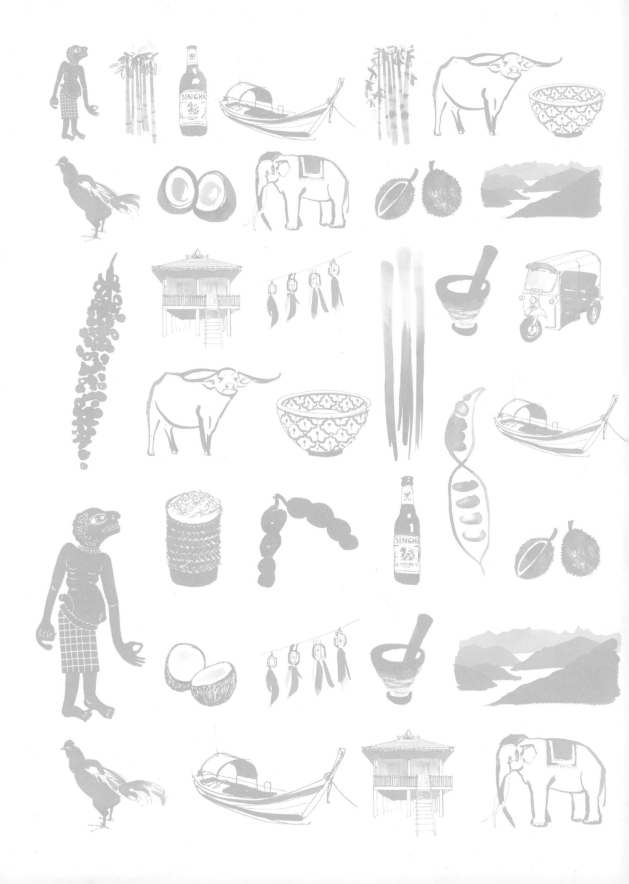